With an Iron Pen

With an Iron Pen

Twenty Years of Hebrew Protest Poetry

Edited by

TAL NITZAN

and

RACHEL TZVIA BACK

excelsior editions

State University of New York Press
Albany, New York

The original Hebrew edition of *With an Iron Pen* was edited by Tal Nitzan; the English edition was edited by Rachel Tzvia Back.

Published by State University of New York Press, Albany

© 2009 State University of New York

Excelsior Editions is an imprint of State University of New York Press

For information, contact State University of New York Press, Albany, NY
www.sunypress.edu

Production by Eileen Meehan
Marketing by Fran Keneston

Library of Congress Cataloging-in-Publication Data

Be-'et barzel. English.
   With an iron pen : twenty years of Hebrew protest poetry / edited by Tal Nitzan and Rachel Tzvia Back.
        p. cm.
   Includes bibliographical references and index.
   ISBN 978-1-4384-2648-8 (pbk. : alk. paper)
   ISBN 978-1-4384-2647-1 (hardcover : alk. paper)
   1. Protest poetry, Hebrew.   2. Israeli poetry.   I. Nitzan, Tal.   II. Back, Rachel Tzvia,
1960–   III. Title.

PJ5042.B4413 2009
892.4'16083581—dc22   2008055003

10 9 8 7 6 5 4 3 2 1

The sin of Judah is written with an iron pen
and with the point of a diamond it is engraved
on the tablet of their heart.

—Jeremiah 17:1

In dark times
Will there also be singing?
Yes, there will also be singing,
About the dark times.

—Bertolt Brecht

Contents

Acknowledgments

(of English Publications Only)

Yehuda Amichai, "And Who Will Remember the Rememberers?" in *Open Closed Open: Poems*, translated by Chana Bloch and Chana Kronfeld (New York: Harcourt, 2000).

Agi Mishol, "Olive Trees" and "To the Muses," in *Look There: New and Selected Poems*, translated by Lisa Katz (Saint Paul, MN: Graywolf, 2006).

Dahlia Ravikovitch, "Free Associating," "The Story of the Arab Who Died in the Fire," and "Lullaby," in *"Hovering at a Low Altitude": The Collected Poetry of Dahlia Ravikovitch*, translated by Chana Bloch and Chana Kronfeld (New York: Norton, 2008).

Aharon Shabtai, "To Dr. Majed Nasser," "Toy Soldiers," "To a Pilot," and "The Reason to Live Here," in *J'Accuse*, translated by Peter Cole (New York: New Directions, 1998).

Meir Wieseltier, "Sonnet: Against Making Blood Speak Out," "The Tel-Aviv Subway," and "Pro & Con," in *The Flower of Anarchy: Selected Poems*, translated by Shirley Kaufman (Berkeley: University of California Press, 2003).

The editors would like to acknowledge the generous support of Dr. Amir Szold, which enabled the publication of the Hebrew version of *With an Iron Pen*.

Preface to the English Edition

Translating and Translocating *With an Iron Pen*

Rachel Tzvia Back

The Israeli occupation of the Palestinian people and their lands in the West Bank entered its fortieth year in June 2007. In those forty years and beyond, thousands of Palestinians have been killed by Israeli military activities, snipers, and settlers. Thousands of houses have been demolished, and tens of thousands of Palestinians live in abject poverty and daily humiliation, with no hope for the future. The occupation has bred a hatred of Israel so deep that young Palestinians, men and women alike, are blowing themselves up in Israeli urban centers; hundreds of innocent Israelis have died in these suicide bombings. The Israeli government has refused to engage in sincere peace talks with the Palestinian authorities and has confiscated hundreds of additional acres of Palestinian lands in the expansion of West Bank Jewish settlements and the building of the "security wall." Relentless despair, hopelessness, and paralysis permeate Palestinian and Israeli societies alike.

In its early years, the occupation was all but invisible to the Israeli Jewish public, whitewashed by the authorities and the media, the oppression obscured by nationalistic propaganda. However, over the last two decades, Israelis in general and artists among them have finally begun to acknowledge the horror of the occupation, its crimes against humanity, and their own blindness—jolted awake primarily by the Palestinian uprisings known as the intifadas.[1] Indeed, a vigorous and vocal protest has ensued, expressing itself also in contemporary Hebrew poetry. This anthology, edited by Israeli poet and translator Tal Nitzan and published in its original Hebrew version by Xargol Books in January 2005, collated those voices of protest and presented them together for the first time.

One may wonder why it took most Hebrew Israeli poets almost twenty years to challenge the consensus and react poetically to the oppressive measures being perpetrated in their names. This delay must be considered also in relation to the role the Hebrew poet has traditionally played in society. Many critics have noted the role of literary culture in the formation of national identities; however, this role cannot be overstated in the case of Israel where Hebrew literary production, expressing an ideology and a hope of nationhood, predated the state by many decades.[2] As Michael Gluzman has argued, from early on Hebrew literature was fiercely engaged in nation building and, consequently, was politicized; indeed, "the literary and political worlds, especially after the shift to Palestine, were entirely intertwined."[3] As such, the Hebrew writer in general—and the Hebrew poet specifically—was expected to speak *for* the nation, in its interests, and in the unified voice of the emerging collective identity. The well-known Hebrew term *shira meguyeset* ("mobilized poetry")—poetry drafted to serve the national agenda—foregrounds how the national agenda itself was often viewed through a prism of militaristic concerns and constructs. Voices of dissent or resistance—voices that dared to consider the plight of the oppressed Arab in Israel's push toward nationhood, security, and power—were marginalized and effectively silenced.

Within this context, the publication of this anthology was a groundbreaking event. Forty-two poets speaking out against their own government's policies—allowing what Wallace Stevens named the "pressure of reality" to inform their poetics—could not be discounted or disregarded. Immediately, the book received accolades from the Israeli press for its daring and beautiful poems, even as it aroused controversy generated by Israeli poets boldly naming the atrocities perpetrated by their government, challenging the near-sacred status of the Israeli soldier, and sometimes examining their own degree of collaboration in the crimes committed in their name. One review called the anthology "a strong and important book,"[4] while another proclaimed that "this anthology is not only an important political act, but above all else an important poetic act."[5] The first edition of the anthology sold out quickly, and a second edition was soon printed.

However, Israel's continuing occupation of the Palestinian people is hardly a regional affair—not emotionally, and not geopolitically. People around the world are engaged in the struggle to bring justice and peace to this region and have, for the most part, been unaware of the vibrant voice of protest among Hebrew poets. Indeed, the majority of the poems in this anthology have never before been published in English translation,[6] and consequently their dissent and their disturbing and powerful poetic images of the continuing Israeli occupation of the West Bank and Gaza[7] have remained inaudible and invisible to all but a Hebrew-speaking audience. To bridge that linguistic gap, to break that silence, and to make these sometimes beautiful, often brutal, poems available also to the English-language audience, an initiative to translate the entire collection and publish it in English began shortly after the publication of the original Hebrew edition and has now reached completion.

This book contains works all originally written in Hebrew, by forty-two poets. For a country as small as Israel, a collection of forty-two different voices provides a wide and impressive reflection of contemporary Hebrew poetry.[8] The poets included in the volume represent a broad range of contemporary Hebrew poets, from preeminent and prize-winning Israeli poets to younger and less well-known poets of Hebrew letters. These poets of protest speak of their shame, rage, despair, and sorrow at the continuing occupation. Each of the nine different sections of the book is devoted to poems that share a particular thematic focus (such as relationship to the land, the death of children, house demolitions). The titles of each section are taken from specific poems in that section.

The translations of these poems were undertaken by eleven different translators—the multiplicity of Hebrew voices appropriately being met by a multiplicity of translating styles. The relationship between poet and translator was similarly diverse. Some of the poets in the anthology worked exclusively with their chosen translator (i.e., Aharon Shabtai with Peter Cole, Meir Wieseltier with Shirley Kaufman), while other poets had their texts conveyed into English by a variety of translators.

The "carrying across" linguistic and cultural borders that is the essence of the translation process[9] is a heightened challenge in the translation of Hebrew texts into English for a variety of reasons. First, the three-letter roots at the base of every Hebrew word establish an intricate relationship even between words that may seem separate and disparate, leading to types of wordplay that are difficult to capture in English. Thus, in Asher Reich's heartbreaking poem "The Observing Heart," which describes a bereaved father visiting his son's grave, the cause of the son's death is never mentioned. However, the poem's repetition of the word *rakav*, "rot," with its root letters *resh-kuf-vav*, evokes the word *kerav*, "battle," with the same root letters, though in a different order (*kuf-resh-vav*). Indeed, the country's military mythology known as *moreshet kerav* (literally "battle legacy," meaning the country's military lore) is here deconstructed and rewritten by Reich as a *moreshet rakav*, an inheritance of deceit and corruption that devours one and all.

A second challenge facing the translator from Hebrew to English is the fashion in which the Old Testament and other Jewish religious and liturgical sources stand as ever-present linguistic and thematic backdrops to both the Hebrew language specifically and Jewish-Israeli culture in general. Consequently, even in these poems written primarily by secular Jewish poets, biblical verses—with their accompanying ancient resonance, register, and morals—together with biblical motifs, figures, and prayers, are alluded to, quoted, and woven into the contemporary poetic landscapes of these texts. The Hebrew-to-English translator must be attentive to these threads ever-present in so many of these poems and their significances to the text. For example, into his terse, haikulike poem which begins "The heart is parched," Tuvia Ruebner inserts the phrase *El maleh rahamim*

("God, full of compassion"), the opening words of the prayer sung for the dead at graveside. The Hebrew reader will immediately recognize the liturgical reference, having heard the prayer recited on every memorial day and at national funerals. Thus the poem in Hebrew evokes the fierce grief of a fresh grave even as it undermines the possibility of comfort through ritual and prayer, for the blood (the poem tells us) is on our hands, and even "God, full of compassion" will *not* forgive "what we have done."

Finally, the act of translation as an act of *translocation*, a change in place, is a relevant and challenging element in the translation of these poems. Indeed, in so many of these poems, the issue of place itself is central, as is the fervent connection *to* a place, a particular land with specific and well-known contours, colors, and fragrances, a land where the olive tree and the grapevine carry ancient and abiding significances. The translator strives to channel these significances to the English-language reader, whose landscapes may differ profoundly from those depicted in the poems. Obviously, the process of lexical and linguistic translocation involves a considerable amount of rupture, even violence—which is wholly appropriate in a collection of poems that confronts the theme of the violent rupturing of the Palestinian people from their land.

In her address on the occasion of her controversial acceptance of the Jerusalem Prize in May 2001, Susan Sontag asserted that "the writer's first job . . . is to tell the truth . . . and refuse to be an accomplice of lies or misinformation." The poets in this collection are truth tellers, at a time and in a place where rampant lies and toxic misinformation continue to lead to abundant human suffering. It is with deep appreciation of this truth telling and admiration of the poetic originality and boldness of this poetry that the translators and editors have worked to bring these poems into English. It is with the belief that a poetic voice may penetrate and influence in places where a theoretical or more conventionally political voice cannot be heard—a belief that the poetic may (again in Sontag's words) "Open up avenues of compassion . . . Remind us that we might, just might, aspire to become different, and better, than we are"—that the anthology *With an Iron Pen: Twenty Years of Hebrew Protest Poetry* is now made available in this English edition.

April 2008

Notes

1. The First Intifada began in December 1987 and continued until September 1993, when Israel and the PLO signed the Declaration of Principles, which began the Oslo Accords. With the collapse of the peace talks, the Second Intifada (also known as the al-Aqsa Intifada, after the al-Aqsa mosque in Jerusalem where it began) erupted in September 2000 and is ongoing. More than 4,700 Palestinians and 1,000 Israelis have already been killed in the al-Aqsa Intifada, in addition to 65 citizens of other countries.

2. See Benjamin Harshav's apt and elegant formulation that Israel is the result of "an ideology that created a language that forged a society that became a state," in Harshav, *Language in Time of Revolution* (Berkley: University of California Press, 1993), p. viii.

3. See Michael Gluzman, *The Politics of Canonicity: Lines of Resistance in Modernist Hebrew Poetry* (Standford: Standford University Press, 2003), p. 7. Gluzman's book is a brilliant examination of the relationship between canon building and national identity formation through an analysis of the specific case of Hebrew poetry.

4. Muki Ron and Hanan Hever in *Haaretz*, Book Supplement, June 15, 2005.

5. David Zonshein in *Haaretz*, Literature and Culture, April 1, 2005.

6. For the list of poems from this anthology that have already been published in book form in English, see publications acknowledgments on page xi.

7. Israel unilaterally disengaged from the Gaza Strip in August 2005. Israeli settlements were dismantled, and the entire Jewish civilian population was moved back within the Green Line. As such, the official Israeli occupation of Gaza ended. However, in effect the Gaza Strip remains under Israeli siege, and Israeli military activity continues there, as does the continual relentless Hamas rocket bombardment of the Israeli towns along the southern border.

8. The adjective *Hebrew* is not synonymous with *Israeli*. The poetic voice of dissent in Israel speaks in many languages that are beyond the purview of this book's exclusive focus on poems of Hebrew-language origin.

9. The word *translate* comes from the Latin translātus, the past participle of *transferre*, "to carry across": *trāns-* "across" + *-lātus*, "carried."

Introduction

"Every Fear, Every Doubt, Every Protest"

Tal Nitzan

Ideological or political poetry in its broad context includes a large range of thematic interests, from straightforward political subjects to poems wherein the "I" itself is a political statement. In contrast, this anthology seeks to narrow the framework, and to track a twenty-year trajectory of Hebrew poetry in its relation to the Israeli oppression of the Palestinian people through the occupation of their lands in the West Bank and the Gaza Strip. In the forty years of its duration, this occupation has penetrated and changed every aspect and realm of Israeli life—including, of course, the realm of poetry.

The previous significant wave of Hebrew protest poetry unfolded in the wake of Israel's incursion into Lebanon in 1982,[1] and those poems were collected in two anthologies: *No End to Battles and Killing* (HaKibbutz HaMeuchad Press, 1983) and *Border Crossing* (Sifriat Poalim, 1983). In several aspects, the situation of those poets was different and, in a fashion, "simpler" than that of poets protesting the occupation: in those poems the poets focused their protest on one specific war, which had at its center a defining trauma—the massacre in the Lebanese refugee camps of Sabra and Shatila in September 1982.[2] In contrast, the Israeli occupation of the West Bank is a multifaceted, multifront phenomenon that has spanned four decades, wherein trauma follows trauma with relentless speed, horror, and frequency. Despite the ever-increasing severity of the war crimes of the occupation, the violence and killing of innocents occur on both sides of the Green Line.[3] The occupied Palestinians also murder innocent Israelis with suicide bombings in civilian centers. As a result, the poetic protest against the occupation is more complicated than the decisive and straightforward poetic protest against the 1982 Lebanon War.

The protest of Hebrew poets is complicated also by the chasm between the message of these poems and the consensus held among the majority of the Jewish Israeli public. Indeed, in the last years a significant change has unfolded in the Israeli public discourse, a change characterized by right-wing extremism and entrenchment in nationalistic views on the one hand and despair and feelings of impotence in the peace camps on the other hand. The historic 400,000-strong Tel-Aviv demonstration against the Lebanon War in September 1982—a protest that took place in the immediate aftermath of the Sabra and Shatila massacre—disintegrated into a much narrower political force in the ensuing years. And even though the peace camp is alive and well in Israel—with the phenomenon of soldiers and reservists refusing to serve in the occupied territories expanding and multiple activist groups aggressively protesting the Separation Wall, the roadblocks and other mechanisms of the occupation—it has become almost commonplace to eulogize the Left and the Israeli peace camps. Of course the poets who wrote against the war in Lebanon did not believe their words would end the war or cause the army to retreat; however, since then, the very concept of 'protest poetry' in Israel has been seen more and more as an isolated and useless cry in the dark. If "high" culture in general, and poetry in particular, has diminished in status, importance, and impact over the last decades, it has seemed as though protest poetry specifically has lost its audience entirely. Even if we do not assume that poets have in their mind's eye at the time of composition both their potential audience and the possibility of influencing that audience, political poetry is inextricably tied to its time and place, and to its readers as well. In certain instances, the addressees not only are implicitly present in the text but are even explicitly named. In his poem "Cry the Beloved Country," for example, Ramy Ditzanny cries out to his compatriots, "my people," saying, "I've seen you in your ugliness debased in your arrogance"; so too Rami Saari states, "Brothers / I'm fed up with [you]" (in "The Only Democracy [in the Middle East]"), and Aharon Shabtai warns his reader, whom he addresses as "my friend," that "tomorrow I'll stand on the porch and see / you, too, crying from the cracks in the backyard pavement" ("Mice of the World, Unite!").

Just when it seems as though there are no more "brothers," "friends," or compatriots to address, one may have expected protest poetry in Israel to fade, if not disappear altogether; yet the opposite has happened, as though the apathy and passivity that have spread through the general Israeli public halted on the threshold of poetry (and other art forms not examined here). Aside from a few exceptions, during the 1980s and into the 1990s, Hebrew poetry protesting the occupation was not prominent in Israeli culture, and, in fact, the majority of Hebrew poetry all but ignored the occupation; however, in the last decade, the necessary and long-awaited moral and literary awakening has occurred, and the phenomenon of protest poetry in Israel has spread. Every year more and more Hebrew poets are writing protest poetry, and this genre of poetry no longer belongs to the so-called "political poets" alone. Alongside poets who have devoted entire books or poem series to protest against the occupation (for example Aharon Shabtai, Ramy Ditzanny, Maxim Gilan, Rami Saari), and alongside poets such as Yitzhak Laor and Meir Wieseltier, for whom political protest has been a primary focus of their poetic oeuvres, there now stand more and more poets who are not necessarily considered "political" but who are producing work addressing the political events of this region in general and the injustice of the occupation specifically. This anthology includes works by forty-two poets, ranging from octogenarian Tuvia Ruebner, who is traditionally identified as a Holocaust generation poet, to Gil Engelstein, a high school student (at the time the anthology was first published); from recipients of the illustrious Israel Prize for Poetry (Dahlia Ravikovitch, Meir Wieseltier, the aforementioned Ruebner) to young poets who have yet to publish their first books; from Salman Masalha, an Israeli-Arab poet who writes in both Hebrew and Arabic, to Yosef Ozer and Dotan Arad who are identified with the Jewish religious poetry journal *Meishiv HaRuach*. The extended silence has at last been broken, and protest against the occupation has become an important, central, and generative subject of contemporary Hebrew poetry.

In a seemingly paradoxical fashion, the poets of this anthology have utilized the obstacles set before them to create a new repertory of techniques, tones, and devices to represent the situation. Thus, the sense of being a minority and impotent before the omnipotent nature of the occupying structure expresses itself in a wide range of tones: sorrow ("a kind of sigh left over from things collapsing in on themselves," Arik A.); lament ("No, no, this is not what we wanted, not this," "Oh, let the darkness cover our eyes!" Tuvia Ruebner); doubt ("my protest lines were all seen as the act of a leftist masturbator / . . . why bother," Ramy Ditzanny); loathing ("with what cement have they filled your heads," Aharon Shabtai); weariness ("the land lies on me / heavy and weary as I am / weary to the bone," Asher Reich); despair ("To where can we still flee from ourselves?" Tuvia Ruebner; "How horrible is this place, our home," Liat Kaplan); and pessimism ("In any case there'll be another war," Dahlia Falah; "And no one will be left all the corpses to tend," David Avidan).

But even when poetry declares its weariness and considers silence an option, the poetic declaration *itself* is a refusal to surrender to fatigue and is a rejection of silence. The ongoing conflict between deep despair and activism expresses itself also in a bitter clarity: Zvi Atzmon dryly declares, at the end of reserve duty in the territories, that "a soldier is a soldier." Against the backdrop of the violence of the occupation, Liat Kaplan expresses disillusion and an awakening from the Zionist dream: "we'll pass by, another anecdote in history's books of forgetting. // From creation's endless circles, existence fleeting // and gone—

I see only bereavement and destruction." The normalization of the occupation's violent methods leads to expressions of alienation and antagonism in many of the poems: "From enemy territory I am writing / ... Like a hostage held / in a sombre city" (Maxim Gilan); "How good it is that I am rid of you, home-land" (Natan Zach); "She's not one of us" (Dahlia Ravikovitch); "My homeland has become for me like a foreign land" (Ramy Ditzanny). But even as several poets separate themselves from the collective identity, primarily by distinguishing between the "I" and the "you" (plural), others continue to speak in the voice of "we": "Do we have time enough for a moral / accounting?" (Moshe Dor); "we still wonder why we insisted on keeping / the human image we've lost" (Rami Saari). And in still other poems the "we" itself is the object of the ironic censure: "That's us, and that's the Tel-Aviv Subway / we dreamed of, united for, dedicated ourselves to" (Meir Wieseltier); "We have a wild need to cause pain / and torture. / For what are we without your agony?" (Dahlia Ravikovitch).

Skeptical protest—protest that is spoken even as it casts profound doubt on its own efficacy—expresses itself most forcefully in the poetry of Meir Wie-seltier, as apparent in his poem "Pro & Con." With a severity that is also self-reflexive, Wieseltier lambastes the three stances from which, according to him, one writes political poetry: the civil, the prophetic, and the ironic. But even after the repeated reproach, "Let there be quiet here," the political poet overcomes the nihilist and returns to his task (however self-critically): "But sometimes I can't control myself, and like a pervert. . . ." In a different text, Wieseltier breaks again the silence he demanded earlier and insists, in a manner free of skepti-cism, that "with necessary wryness I must say that also in times of pain one must sharpen the truth."

The skepticism of "Pro & Con" is absent from other poems, which adopt an unapologetic, even prophetic, tone. In several poems by Ramy Ditzanny, for example, the tone and lexis are indubitably prophetic. Ditzanny's poem "Cry the Beloved Country" recreates the biblical prophecies of destruction, leaving no room for satire or parody. The pathos of this poem climaxes in the final lines: "Therefore, behold—/ the days are coming"—a biblical verse repeated in the Old Testament books of Isaiah, Jeremiah, and Amos, a verse that is here fragmented and aborted, as though the speaker's voice has broken at the climactic moment and cannot go on. Thus, ironically, the poem of prophecy offers no prophecy at all. For those familiar with the biblical texts, what resounds in the silence are the prophets' dire predictions of exile and destruction: "Therefore, behold, the days are coming when everything in your palace ... will be carried off to Baby-lon; nothing will be left behind" (Isaiah 39:6), and, "Assuredly the day is coming, declares the Lord, when this place shall no longer be called Topheth or Valley of Ben-Hinnom, but the Valley of Slaughter" (Jeremiah 19:6). One may see in the aborted ending Ditzanny's self-reproach over the pointless effort of speaking to the conscience of "fellow men" whose "ears are closed to the outcry of the oppressed"; however, an alternative and darker reading of this truncated ending may see it as an implicit statement that those prophecized days of destruction and despair have, in fact, already arrived.

Aharon Shabtai also writes in this ancient tone of chastisement, free of hesitancy and postmodern ambivalence. In "Toy Soldiers," for example, sentence after sentence ends in an accusatory question mark addressed toward the clearly defined "you," the "Idiotic soldiers of lead." If there is sarcasm or mockery here, it is not directed at the speaker or at his naiveté in moralizing in a cynical age, but rather at the eponymous subject whose brains, apparently, contain not "even an ounce of imagination." Shabtai's unstinting commitment to this poetic protest expresses itself also in his willingness to use the aforementioned aggressive punctuation that exposes not only the rhetorical mechanism of the poem but also its highly emotional and ethical stand and leaves the text—and its author—vulnerable to the danger of ridicule and disregard.

Another type of rigorous poetic protest, which may be defined as the poetics of empathy, expresses itself in this collection in poems of mourning and rage over the Palestinian victims of the occupation—victims who are invisible and nameless to the military forces, the governing structures, and a large part of the public and the media. This stance is dominant in the work of Dahlia Ravikovitch, one of the first Israeli poets who refused the national monopoly on bereavement, resisted any hierarchy of suffering or distinction between victims, and consistently and vigorously protested both the usage of "our" (as in, Israeli) dead as a justification for war and the glorification of death as holy and heroic. One cannot overstate the degree of resistance apparent in this type of poetry, which goes beyond compassion and identification with the victims. The oppression of another people necessitates a denial of their humanity; thus, empathy toward that same people is dangerous and forbidden, for it might undermine the certainty of the finger on the trigger or the foot on the bulldozer's pedal. Indeed, the subversiveness of these poems expresses itself in their insistence on foregrounding the humanity and humanness of "the enemy." These texts of poetic empathy focus fiercely on the individual, the face and name behind a statistic quickly forgotten from the collective memory: not "a minor" or a "terrorist" (at ten years of age) or just an anonymous "Palestinian" who "met his death," but Nur Ismail, Ali Joarish, Hilmi Shusha. In protest against the cynical phrase "details of the event are unknown" regularly utilized in official announcements, these poems insist on investigating and knowing those details.

These poets who deal in "current events" must contend with an additional obstacle: the dense and relentless "routine" of the occupation. Like a disease whose symptoms are many and varied, the pathological reality of the occupation strikes daily. An event, followed by a response-to-the-event, followed by retribution-for-the-response, followed by revenge-for-the-retribution, is the implacable and unforgiving formula: in Tuvia Ruebner's words, "A victim begets a victimizer, victimizer begets a knife / a knife begets fear, fear / begets hatred, hatred—wickedness ..." Every time it seems as though the horror has reached its peak, has played itself out, another "incident" happens, proving that greater extremes are still to come. The poetry, however, does not relent as it struggles to represent this wild, unwieldy, and rapidly changing reality. In fact in many cases the poetic response comes in tandem with the events themselves, as they occur (the Separation Wall and the poetic response to it, even as it is being constructed, being a case in point).

One of the strategies for dealing with the intensity of the situation is by addressing and "attacking" it indirectly, through other texts. Of course, intertextuality is hardly the creation of Hebrew protest poets; still, a unique and multifaceted use of this technique is apparent in this collection. Several poems open a dialogue with other texts. For example, in "From the Songs of Tu B'Shevat," Avner Treinin transforms a popular children's folk song for the Israeli festival of tree planting into a poem about burying bodies (in holes dug for the saplings). In "We'll Build Our Homeland, for This Land Is Ours," Ramy Ditzanny uses the refrain from a Zionist folk song as the ironic title for his poem describing the dispossessed and disempowered Palestinians who are, in fact, the ones building "our Greater Land of Israel."

In his poem "Language," Natan Zach confronts not another poem but rather the fashion in which the occupation has bastardized language itself. He exposes the injustices, cruelties, and lies hiding behind the dangerous euphemisms of military-speak and political spinning. Similarly, Zvi Atzmon attacks the insidious acronyms of military language in his poem "The Letters' Rebellion": "N.S.B. stands for Non-Standard Baton— / any handle of a shovel—efficient, don't worry." But even in the context of the seemingly neutral and intentionally emotionless military terminology, words such as *burning* and *terror* proclaim themselves and jump to the foreground.

While many texts are alluded to in these poems, the single text that is most often present, in some form or another, is, of course, the Old Testament. Thus, Tuvia Ruebner's desperate cry that "it was our hands that spilt our blood!" is taken almost word for word from Deuteronomy (21:7), but the assertion of innocence in the biblical verse ("It was *not* our hands that shed this blood") becomes an admission of guilt in Ruebner's text, through the change of a single letter. The phrase itself is taken from a ritual of repentance and cleansing necessary when one finds a murdered body and the murderer is unknown. In Ruebner's text, however, the murderer is known: it is "us." Moreover, the blood being spilled is *also* our own. Thus Ruebner links the sin to its punishment.

Yitzhak Laor's poem "Order of the Day" illustrates how the phrase "Remember what Amalek has done unto you" (Deuteronomy 25:17) has been transformed into the Jewish justification for any and all its deeds: the memory of Amalek's cruelty serves to perpetuate the Jewish people's eternal victimhood and makes oppression of another people—anywhere and at any time—just and necessary. The message is refined to its essence in Laor's poem, which states: "If you can't find yourself / an Amalek, call /Amalek whomever / you want to do / to him what / Amalek did, / to you of course." Similarly, in her poem "At the Edges of the East," Oreet Meital addresses the self-righteousness of the eternal victim—a foundational principle of Israeli policy and identity—by inverting biblical terms. Thus, the "garrisoned cities" of Exodus are no longer the cities the enslaved Israelites built for the pharaohs in Egypt but rather the Israeli cities of contemporary Israel being built by Palestinian laborers.

Many of this collection's poems change biblical figures into Palestinian ones: Aryeh Sivan transforms the biblical boy Joseph who went to Shechem (the modern-day Palestinian city of Nablus) to tend his sheep into "a different beautiful boy / from Shechem," a murdered Palestinian boy with a hole in his chest "not from the teeth of a wild beast" but from a bullet. Yosef Ozer compares Ali Joarish, who was fatally wounded by a rubber bullet, to Ishmael expelled into the desert, but it is not an angel of God who appears before Ali Joarish, as appeared once before Ishmael, but rather the Angel of Death.

Variations on biblical verses expose also the gap between the divine promise regarding the Promised Land, and the defective reality, proving the falseness of the promise itself. Asher Reich transforms the "the land flowing with milk and honey" into "a land flowing with darkness and deceit," and Rami Saari quotes a verse about a beloved son who won God's mercy—"Truly, Ephraim is a darling son to Me, a child that is dandled" (Jeremiah 31:20)—in order to protest this son's contemporary, merciless, and violent version: "And my darling son, with a club and rubber bullets."

Biblical metamorphoses that measure the distance between the vision and its harsh reality are embedded also in Aharon Shabtai's "The Fence" where biblical sources evolve into the dark and terrible details from the daily reality of the occupation. Thus, the speaker lifts his eyes to the hills (Psalms 121:1), but instead of asking, "From whence comes my help?" he asks simply, "And what do I see?" The answer "Cube after cube of evil"—alluding to the concrete slabs of the Separation Wall—replaces the belief that "my help cometh from the Lord, who made Heaven and Earth" (Psalms 121:2). This same "heaven"—or sky—appears at the end of the poem, offering no protection as it is itself cursed ("rooftops curse the sky"), and the name of God himself is replaced in this poem with the explicit and various names of evil: iniquity, dispossession, oppression, thievery, and malice.

Like a map of 1:1 scale, the most extreme use of biblical texts is apparent in the poems that integrate the biblical into the texts, without addition or commentary and almost without adaptation. Thus, in "Now Is the Time," Liat Kaplan weaves fragments of biblical verses on revenge (from Exodus 21) through her poem, adapting the verses only by changing their order, transforming a singular first-person voice into a plural first-person and adding a title. Zvi Atzmon goes even further and composes a poem, "With the Steel Point of a Thorn," entirely from biblical descriptions of destruction taken from the prophecies of Isaiah and Jeremiah, adding no interpretation aside from the new juxtaposition of these phrases. In both cases, the poets minimize their role to directing our gaze at the ancient words, with the power of the statement emanating from this poetic asceticism.

However, within the context of this extensive use of intertextuality, one must emphasize that the texts alluded to—whether an earlier poem, a lexical term, or a biblical verse—are never the objective or focus of the poem but rather serve as a doorway to the real subject, the occupation. The poems are relentless in their gaze on this reality: the oppression and cruelty, the refugee camps, the killing of children, the daily abuse of people with roadblocks and curfews, the terror, and the danger of complete destruction that is intrinsic to the continuing occupation.

Indeed, the awareness that within the occupation resides, also, the seed of the destruction of the State of Israel itself is declared in many poems: "on the land of my people / briers will rise up" (Zvi Atzmon); "From the hill / where we stood, you can see / the secrets of destruction" (Rami Saari); "the tanks murdering / in my name are digging a grave for my people as well" (Aharon Shabtai), and more. Of course, the repeated references to the prophecies of destruction are hardly arbitrary. The tragedy in these poems, as in the biblical prophecies, emanates from the fact that awareness of the destruction that undoubtedly lies in wait is inextricably bound up in the knowledge of one's impotence to prevent it from coming: "I've wasted words / . . . this ugly madness can not be stopped" (Ramy Ditzanny).

Certainly, "paper fighter planes" cannot penetrate "steel and bulletproof glass" (Meir Wieseltier), and words cannot "send a shiver through a sniper's finger" (Aharon Shabtai, nor halt the violence, transform the hatred, or bring about peace. Then what is the purpose—the *raison d'etre*—of the poems collected here? What reason is there to write these words if the march of oppression, based on blindness, arrogance, and callousness continues to reign supreme? Part of the answer to the question is found in the poems themselves: "I have no choice / but to resist," writes Yitzhak Laor. As such, the question why or what for has no relevance here. Literary opposition exists even in places where the price for it is higher than disregard or slander. Besides its literary and documentary value, protest poetry grants its reader a foothold for resistance in a time and place where resistance is rare, pushed to the margins, deemed unacceptable. Before a ruling authority whose "horrible self-righteous scream" increases the more it tramples every hope for peace "with a steel leg" (in Natan Zach's words), before official propaganda that whitewashes catastrophic, destructive, and immoral policies, a conformist media that, by and large, omits from its reports "every fear, every doubt, every protest" (in Aharon Shabtai's phrase), poetry becomes a rebellious act that unsettles axioms, generates question marks, and asserts the right of readers and writers as one to doubt, protest, and rise up.

Therefore, the importance of protest poetry in general, and this collection of Hebrew protest poetry specifically, cannot be measured in quantitative or practical terms. The impression that this poetry imprints in the minds and hearts of the public can be seen mostly only from the distance of time. The ethical stand taken by the poets and poems of this anthology represents today the minority position—a minority that is seen by the majority of the Jewish Israeli public as "self-hating" and as desecrators of sacred ideals. And still, throughout history, literary creations have expressed the forbidden and the revolutionary and have preceded—in fact, precipitated—changes in attitudes and societal norms. The day will come when the poems collected in *With an Iron Pen* will be read as the voice of reason and of honest hearts in dark times.

(Translated from the Hebrew by Rachel Tzvia Back)

Notes

1. In the summer of 1982, Israel launched a massive attack to destroy all military bases of the PLO in southern Lebanon and, after a ten-week siege on the Muslim sector of West Beirut and the PLO stronghold there, forced the Palestinians to accept a U.S.-sponsored plan whereby the PLO guerrillas would evacuate Beirut and go to several Arab countries that had agreed to accept them. Israel withdrew from Lebanon in 1985 but continued to maintain a Lebanese-Christian policed buffer zone north of its border, until its final withdrawal from all territories in southern Lebanon in 2000.

2. On September 16, 1982, in a region occupied by the Israeli army, Lebanese Christian militiamen entered Beirut's Sabra and Shatila refugee camps, bent on revenge for the assassination of their leader, Bashir Gemayel. There followed a three-day massacre during which hundreds of innocent civilians were killed.

3. The "Green Line" refers to the demarcation between the 1967 borders of Israel and the West Bank territories captured in the Six-Day War. Although usually referred to as the "1967 border," it is actually the 1949 armistice line, as there was no internationally recognized border at the time. The Green Line reference came about because someone used a green pen on the map of the armistice agreement with Jordan to draw the border. Most of the peace talks between Israeli and Palestinian authorities have been based on the premise that Israel must retreat to the Green Line in order to allow the Palestinians to establish their own nation east of this border.

I

And the Land, Will You Possess It All?

In Enemy Territory / Maxim Gilan

From enemy territory I am writing
coded messages, writing as though
to the resistance. Like a hostage held
in a sombre city, loving the enemy.

I write here and they say *sit there*—
I write there and they say *soon*—
ripping up the words, and not just them,
setting lyrics to a graceless tune.

I write in sorrow. Sometimes hatred
descends on my palate as at a feast of riches
a stew of revenge and reverence
before what might have been here, once.

I write also in happiness, but not gloating.
I write with precision, I write as a witness.
Not part of the fair. Representative exhibit.
Present-absentee. Most unfashionably.

But also as a returnee,
looking hard all around
with vain hope I see
the enemy everywhere. Even in me.

Translated by Rachel Tzvia Back

Cry the Beloved Country / Ramy Ditzanny

I cry for my people who have no heart of their own with which to cry:
I've seen you in your ugliness debased in your arrogance
an assembled mob crowd pre-nation—
a nation not of brethren not together not benevolent
a nation with no love of humankind.
My homeland has become like a foreign land where I walked with shame
I've become strange to my compatriots
I've become quarrelsome, contentious—
a bitter, beaten man. I've become loathsome to myself.

You returned to the sheltering land your forefathers already despaired of—
and will you drive forth those
who escaped the sword?
You've relied on your sword,
you've committed a multitude of abominations,
your ears are closed to the outcry of the oppressed—
and the land, will you possess it all?

Therefore, behold—
the days are coming

Translated by Rachel Tzvia Back

Palestina—Eretz Yisrael / Arik A.

In the beginning of 2001
while I was playing with my little boy in the living room
the television reported an earthquake in western
India; immediately I switched channels, lest we feel
the shaking.
As if the earth hadn't trembled,
we kept on;
as if it hasn't already been cracked for months.

It got late, time for beddy bye,
but in the room, disharmony—
a kind of sigh left over from things collapsing in on themselves.

The next day, the delight of sunrise
almost made us forget,
and I did everything I could to keep on
the regular course,
but in the evening, the television turned off, I noticed it
escalating and grating on our ears,
piling up like a tower of toys here
in the ex-Mandate, Palestina—Eretz Yisrael:
the despairing cry of grave-diggers over
the silence of the buried,
and one can already see the crack which has formed—
even while I'm still holding
my little boy—
in the shell that covers us as
we keep on

Translated by Rachel Tzvia Back

[Palestinian souls] / Dotan Arad

1.
Palestinian souls
are dancing on my balcony
under the white crescent moon
dancing and never touching
keeping a safe distance
leaving pale footprints
on the tiles

Salaam aleikum
Aleikum salaam
(three times)

Palestinian souls are standing behind the walls
looking for the cracks

2.
Palestinian souls
are hiding in my house
behind the furniture
the white-washers of words can't
erase their fingerprints
from the paint.
Their suitcases are on their knees,
they're waiting for a sign.

3.
The souls of Palestinians are thickening
                                multiplying
Woven in secret
from the lettered codes
on the radio
already they stand before me
bloodless and boneless
without flesh or limbs
playing words for me in classical Arabic,
plucking on the strings of my guilt.

I take them for a walk in the garden.
Don't forget to prune the cherry tree
and don't sit under the vine
in pretend peace
This house is built on arches
Beware
Smash all your dreams
with an axe
and collect the word-shells
from the ground

Lest you pay the price of exile.

Translated by Rachel Tzvia Back

We'll Build Our Homeland, for This Land Is Ours / Ramy Ditzanny

Unlucky minors are building homes for their carefree neighbors;
cursing, rolling home-grown tobacco, spitting at distances pissing
on the fortified concrete, clogging up the plumbing when the contractor is
   away,
building in order to destroy building hopelessly.

For in the resentment of impotence, in the pain of resignation
with straw-mixed bricks, the many-storied buildings are being built
in our Greater-Land-of-Israel—
and the pneumatic drills pound pound pound in fury.

And in the fields thousands of *falahim*, sheaf to sheaf, declare:
We will stay true to every clod of earth!
Our cousins are building hating building—
our Greater-Land-of-Israel they are building:

Wait! We'll grow a little, then we'll blow up the buildings
in every garrisoned city now being built in the heart of hatred—
Then, stone for a stone blow for blow we'll smash your heads
against the witnessing wall, a monument to Our Greater Land.

Translated by Rachel Tzvia Back

Mice of the World, Unite! / Aharon Shabtai

On TV they're showing a baby dying of hunger in Zaire,
so that we'll learn, be shaped, adjust,
so we'll swallow still one more entertainment-pill
and, without the cornea thickening like a sole,
shed a tear, but salute the hunters and seekers of prey.
Therefore they show the soldier sitting on a dusty knoll
and lavishing, with a chilling naiveté, praise on the virtues of his dog.
He's sent to serve as a model, as he sinks his teeth
into the kaffiyehed rabbit-man darting about in the grove.
And here's our friend, the bulldozer, rattling onto the screen—
through confiscated lots of miserable people—
and biting into the olive trees.
The screen is a blackboard for teaching the novice
to eliminate all doubt, timidity, and restraint;
the bulldozer's needed for the maintenance
of sanitary standards within the environment—
like a tanker for the draining of sewage, or a truck for garbage.
Those in uniform, beating women by the checkpoint,
and the helicopter hovering above the refugee camp,
as though it were dusting a field,
are engaging in the eradication
of a new kind of pest that has spread.
And as the few grow richer,
more and more people are turned into rats
and mice, into useless creatures, refuse,
backed into quarters, ghettos, prisons—
blacks, Thais, Arabs, etcetera.
But wait, my friend: tomorrow I'll stand on the porch and see
you, too, squeaking from the cracks in the backyard pavement
and from your burrows in the vacant lot: "Mice of the world, unite!"

Translated by Peter Cole

The Only Democracy (in the Middle East) / Rami Saari

This won't be a political poem, brothers,
I'm fed up
with Cowboys and Indians,
and Cops and Robbers.
Are these really the young men
who were supposed to play before us,
petting Palestinian forces with mortar fire?
And my darling son, with a club and rubber bullets?

What can I say? The movie is fascinating
even if most of us have minor parts;
we still hope
to win, like men, a big win:
eating, gorging, consuming everything
like live fire, the human image in God's image,
like idolaters ardently worshipping
a Biblical whore, a temple prostitute, a furrow of earth, a city of fools;
the Wild West
settles in ancestral graves
here in the east.

Translated by Lisa Katz

The Horizon's Clenched Mouth / Liat Kaplan

"Did the cicada shell sing itself utterly away?" Its cocoon is buried
in the ground seventeen years, lives one hour and is devoured.
Will we be silent until we become muteness?

Meanwhile we are ensconced in our homes. The streets are empty. The beach
alone is crowded. All the birds are crows, landing on their own shadows.
The sea is wide, green, glittering in vain.

In the horizon's clenched mouth, the last orange light of day hides. Time
has cracked here. A sudden rain pours down. Yellow bursts forth
from the land of Palestine: chrysanthemums, oxalis,

mustard, sunflowers, fennel, marigolds, groundsels, and sun. Tomorrow
the blossoming will turn into summer's stubble and we'll pass by,
another anecdote in history's books of forgetting.

News of the invasion into Balata and gunshots at the station. Now the evening
primroses flower at the Memorial for Fallen Sons.
From creation's endless circles, existence fleeting

and gone, I see only bereavement and destruction. This is spring.
We do not know it. A beloved land, enraged, devours us. Day by day
the darkness is fresh, as certain as sunset.

One cannot bathe in the same blood twice. The body dims, only it
exists now. Like the sea, like the sea. And there's no lifeguard

                    Did she cry herself utterly away?

Translated by Rachel Tzvia Back

Free Associating / Dahlia Ravikovitch

What does she have to say?
What does she have to say?
What else has she got to say?
She's got a perverted desire for suffering.
Well, in our country we have such beautiful landscapes,
vineyards perched on the mountainside,
the shadow of clouds on the plain
and light
and a fenced-in plot of land;
and three rows of olive trees too,
uprooted as a punitive measure.
And three old women, their teeth rooted out.
Because of old age, of course, what else?
Violence isn't everything.
Why, of all things, on a bright clear Sabbath,
a perfectly happy Sabbath,
does the memory of that man
have to sneak up again, the one they beat to death?
Ye shall not kill that man and his son both in one day.

The blot of a light cloud
has settled down in the plain.
In Zikhron Ya'akov, the vineyards are bursting
with the nectar of grapes.
Our storehouses are filled with grain,
our wadis with water,
but turn over any stone
and out creeps a scorpion.
The Song of Nature.
And that Arab they beat to death.
Actually broke his body with their blows.
But not in Zikhron Ya'akov
and not in Mazkeret Batya,
those sleepy old towns of the Baron de Rothschild
that blend so nicely into the landscape.

What does she have to say?
What does she have to say?
She's just looking for ways to suffer,

to say a bad word.
She's not one of us,
She can't see what's good and beautiful in life.
She won't see us the way we are.
Anu banu artza:
We Came to Build the Land.

Translated by Chana Bloch and Chana Kronfeld

II

The Arrogance of
Our Self-Destruction

A Small Song for the Fallen / Natan Zach

How good it is that I am rid of you,
of your tyranny,
of your clamorous demands,
of the never-ending harassment,
the self-righteousness
that looks out only for itself,
is always right in its own eyes,
self-justification
that won't quit,
won't stop
years after I am done,
years after I am gone,
when there is no man left
that I have known
and no woman left
whose body has
lain down with mine.

The grandeur of the future in its every utterance
which both asks and answers,
the horrors of the past at its feet
and its eyes cast up to the heights
with a fearful cry for help
demanding comfort
as it stomps with a steel foot
all who stand in its way,
all who cross its path,
all who were its sons,
how good it is that I am rid of you, My Homeland.

Translated by Mark Braverman

Asteroid / Moshe Dor

> An asteroid is falling toward Earth
> and may hit it in thirty years.
> —*Washington Post*, November 2000

At the elevation of five steps above
the ground I take a good position
from which I can watch the world: a wind shakes
the last of the withered leaves from
the branches of the deciduous trees. The sky
is clear of falling stars. And at a distance large
enough to stay uninvolved, Beit Ja'ala
is shooting at Gilo, and Gilo is returning fire.

Do we have time enough for a moral
accounting? Or perhaps we've seen enough
movies on the destruction of the universe from the direct
hit of a meteor in order to be hardened and refuse to rescind
the arrogance of our self-destruction?

Leaves whirl around my head like a wreath
or a halo, and when you come out to the balcony
to tell me, Beit Ja'ala is shooting at
Gilo, and Gilo is returning fire,
I, from my observation point
of five steps above the ground, know
that I am involved up to my neck and that the asteroid will
hit its target, if not in 30 years
then in its own time and place, when it sees fit.

Translated by Rachel Tzvia Back

Sonnet: Against Making Blood Speak Out / Meir Wieseltier

If I die one day from the bullet of a young killer—
a Palestinian who crosses the northern border—
or from the blast of a hand grenade he throws,
or in a bomb explosion while I'm checking the price
of cucumbers in the market, don't dare say
that my blood permits you to justify your wrongs—
that my torn eyes support your blindness—
that my spilled guts prove it's impossible
to talk with them about an arrangement—that it's only possible
to talk with guns, interrogation cells, curfew, prison,
expulsion, confiscation of land, curses, iron fists, a steel heart
that thinks it's driving out the Amorites, destroying the Amalekites.
    Let the blood seep into the dust; blood is blood, not words.
    Terrible—the illusion of the Kingdom in obtuse hearts.

Translated by Shirley Kaufman

from Israeli Thoughts / Asher Reich

1.
I am under myself
and the land lies under me
deader and more dead
as I am daily.

The heart remembers other days
when the land was a language
our new history
resting in her sickbed
with burn marks on her skin.

In my sleep the land lies on me
heavy and weary as I am,
weary to the bone. Still I dream
about another land that looks
just like my land use to
at its beginning
and I wake, trembling within, and lost.

2.
I remember their shape vaguely,

the exalted dead of
our new history—

their spilt blood brought
no savior.
I wonder how they are now

looking at this land
where we've all been killed.
A land flowing with darkness and deceit,
concealing the future as with a *tallit*.

Translated by Rachel Tzvia Back

Language / Natan Zach

Confirming a Kill	—	A bullet to the head
Exposing the Enemy	—	Uprooting olive groves
Collateral Damage	—	Every neighbor's life imperiled
Encirclement	—	A city under siege
Closure	—	Jailing civilians in their homes
Targeted Eliminations	—	Killing the good with the bad
Administrative Detention	—	Imprisonment without trial
Bargaining Chips	—	Toying with human life
Roadblocks	—	Breaking a people's spirit
Delimiting Village Expansion	—	Banishing a man to the wilderness
Family Unification Plan	—	Separating husbands from their wives
Trial	—	Distinguishing between blood and blood
Emigration Directorate	—	Arresting men in their sleep
Human Resource Company	—	Robbing the foreigner of his livelihood
Urban Development	—	Building new prisons
Settlement Outposts	—	Deluding the world
An Isolationist Nation	—	Sonic booms over neighboring countries
Geneva Accords	—	The murder of a seven-year-old boy

Translated by Rachel Tzvia Back

[Lice have conquered you] / Tuvia Ruebner

Lice have conquered you, glorious Holy Land.
And they've sucked your blood. Everyone has failed.
What's been done cannot be undone. Weep and wail.
For you've ceded all rule and command to the parasites.

Translated by Rachel Tzvia Back

Khan Younis / Tal Nitzan

The cat will be scolded and banished to the balcony,
the scratch on my child's hand will be kissed,
but your little boy knows terrors
no kiss can wipe away.
Pride of the family! He is only two years old
and already knows
how to warn his mother
to crouch down
when the shots fly into the house.
"The window through which the wind creeps—
close it now and lie down to sleep"
you quote, but
our efficient bullets penetrate doors, walls,
window-panes. Now the bullet-riddled sign on which
you naively wrote:
ש'إنتبهوا ! ؛ عائلات تسكن هنا!
!انه نكست تالئاع ! اوهبتنإ!
Attention! Families live here!
sways in the wind
while from the perforated boilers, water
runs down the house's cheeks.

Translated by Rachel Tzvia Back

Woodcut of a Landscape / Dvora Amir

From the peak of Mount Scopus, peace unto you Esaweya—
peace to your dust and to your picturesque landscape,
etched in the valley as in a Bezalel bowl.
Shepherds from the days of Anatot drive their sheep on the slope
and a girl, jug on her head, dances toward the well.
Ancient pastoralism terrifies my heart,
for evil will emerge from it, and God's word is absent.
From the delivery room window the mother of the newborn hears
a bulldozer rumbling, a house collapsing, a gunshot, ruptured screams.
So it will be done—killing in the name of the law.
When they bring the baby to her, she asks
alarmed: "Is something wrong?"
"Everything is fine," the doctor calms her, "his lungs are mature,
he'll breathe on his own."

Translated by Rachel Tzvia Back

At the Edges of the East / Oreet Meital

Someone must know that the sweet blood of slaves is being poured into
    shattered goblets
in the wretched cities, where the refuse of hope is tossed upon heaps of ruins
and bleary-eyed children crawl in the streets, searching
for blood pecking at rationed hope tick ticking between saboteur bricks
    behind ruined walls
chiseling at hope and bursting out round-eyed as bombs
they do not distinguish between friend and foe, they are not content
with the edges of our pale fingers stretching out toward peace
in the garrisoned cities crossed fingers returning empty, there
they crawl in the streets seeking blood spilled
in vain picking up beautiful garbage throwing it down garbage rolling in the
    streets
someone must know that they are rising up in the streets and gathering
and they cannot distinguish between true enemies and us

and the eyes of the masters are sunk deep into their backs
on the sides of their heads rolling back haunted
they never sleep
and muscled masters walk in the streets changing
Holocaust into Heroism
with all their might they will not surrender the horror
they teach their young children the sword
so they'll know war no more, they teach
forgetting in the short term and remembering for the long term
they lick the blood of slaves sweet from goblets
shattered on the beach, they sink
into the sinking sun, their skewed eyes are blind
and in their ears, sealed to the sound of the waves,
all outcries are swallowed up.

Translated by Rachel Tzvia Back

Thursday at Angel's Bakery / Dahlia Falah

All night long a high school student from Ramallah braids challah bread
at a Jewish bakery. Friday morning rises sevenfold more secular
with the concerns of preparing for Sabbath sanctity. The bakery van arrives,
slanted wheat-stalk on its caulked doors cut in half when the doors open.
The challah loaves are hot and burn his palms. He catches and tosses them
as they roll down, shiny with egg veneer, golden with sesame seeds.
Birds sing from the rooftops above the almond trees.
The children on vacation gather rocks to throw at the Jewish soldiers.

Translated by Rachel Tzvia Back

The Night after the Surgeries / Dahlia Falah

This is the night after the surgeries:
everyone is lying sedated with morphine,
and the screws extracted from them
have been transferred to the Secret Service.
As usual, everything is closed up there
in the hospital—just as the operating rooms
are closed, and the extracted nails and screws
are sealed up in a special evidence bag,
in case the Secret Service expresses an interest in them,
in case they want to know from which
village hardware store
they were taken
to fulfill their purpose.

Translated by Rachel Tzvia Back

The Tel-Aviv Subway / Meir Wieseltier

Beautiful and virtual—
that's the Tel-Aviv Subway.
Bizarre, sprawling far
through a vastness that pinches our hearts.
Buried in mountains and valleys
she glows inaudibly,
our one-of-a-kind dream train,
flies incandescent in blood-red,
in asphalt-black, in concrete-gray,
and an airy opaque white,
the ancient color of human bones.
Because she was pieced together
out of odd parts:
reinforced concrete from fortifications,
Jerusalem stone, bypass roads,
red roof tiles, human bones.
Bones of our brothers, our children, bones of our cousins.
That's us, and that's the Tel-Aviv Subway
we dreamed of, united for, dedicated ourselves to.
Perhaps this secret subway of ours
spreads out a little too thin
over sites evacuated in the Sinai desert, over the splendid hills
that roll between Jenin and Hebron.
Some naysayers might claim it's too hard
to fit an escalator
in a subway like that.
So what? She's ours,
and there's no other like her on earth.

Translated by Shirley Kaufman

A Prayer to Allah Hashem God / David Avidan

A prayer to Allah Hashem in the Heavens, Ruler Above—
we've come to you God, shadow of death's death, for love.
We are low miserable foul dwellers in dust—
we are still here and have been from first dusk.
We are walking to the terminal edge of the end—
and no one will be left all the corpses to tend.

Translated by Rachel Tzvia Back

III

The Fruit Dies Before the Tree

[This is not what we wanted] / Tuvia Ruebner

This is not what we wanted, no, no, not this.
Without them, who are we and for what?
We didn't want this, no, not this, we didn't think it would be like this:
how the land just devours and devours.

Translated by Rachel Tzvia Back

Mite / Aryeh Sivan

After the fiftieth killed and the two hundred and twentieth wounded
the news stories about the ones that come after are like flies,
not even the flies of the dead, those coating
the window-panes and screens.

Only an exceptional occurrence like
the eight-month-old baby whose face
was shattered by a rubber bullet or the old Arab
who was beaten to death two or three times
after he was already dead, only an event like that
becomes a worthy news item
like an angry locust or a restless bee
sketching broken circles around our heads.

Until suddenly, in the heat wave of a spring day,
a Jew sits down to dinner with his family
and his house fills up, as though on its own, with flies
hundreds of small flies
on the dishes and in the food on their eyes
ears and lips—

and if a person completely seals all his orifices
how will he taste or enjoy
anything

until the wind returns, blowing from the West

Translated by Rachel Tzvia Back

Torn / Tal Nitzan

At night he comes to me,
the boy from the scorched bus.
He is torn from me, again and again
as his hands are torn from him, and his legs,
and I'm his mother.
A quick word
                    mother
Maybe it was cut off in his mouth
when he was swallowed by fire.
All night long I try to bring him back
to his childhood
where he knew how to take comfort
in my kisses on every blow and bruise.
By morning the radio bird
rises from a car to my window
to screech revenge:
They shot or didn't shoot,
a shell or maybe not,
into the kitchen or onto a cot
unto the third generation or maybe fourth,
two kids (what were they doing there anyway)
or just a pregnant woman,
a deaf old man or a blind soldier—
Now arise, get thee out
from nightmare to nightmare.

Translated by Tal Nitzan, with Vivian Eden

Ballad for an Old Palestinian / Dvora Amir

The soul is a black forest
the soul is a stone on the crossbar of a well
suspended between two worlds.

By day a downy cloud seals the roof of his house. By night
the moon rests on it like a silver jewel on holiday wrapping.
Early in the morning the old man leaves the village,
"The autumn leaves have again painted the sparrows' wings
yellow and orange," he thinks.
He wonders, how does the tree know itself in borrowed colors.
Through naked groves, over stone terraces, he walks to his abandoned village
where he'll meet a few old spirits, friends.

Today it is told among the hills—his grandson was shot.
On a stretched canvas,
on a bed of twigs the boy's body is tossed about.
Evacuated, as one wounded in battle, to a hidden gathering place.
His body is jolted upward, swaying on the storm of mourners,
lifted up, brought down, and again floating above as though wanting to rise
toward the sky.
"I had a grandson, small, one, mine.
I had a grandson, a dreaming boy. With my own eyes I saw how he stood
with closed eyes before the mirror, watching himself dream."

The soul is a black forest
the soul is a stone on the crossbar of a well
suspended between two worlds.

Translated by Rachel Tzvia Back

To Dr. Majed Nassar / Aharon Shabtai

The e-mail hasn't stopped for a minute. For three
days now, like a foul wave, a pogrom
has been sweeping over six towns. Donations
of blood were gathered by a doctor from Beit Sahour

for Bethlehem's wounded, but they can't get through.
Tanks have surrounded the hospital, and so, instead,
straight from Manger Square, they've brought him a dead
boy killed by an army sniper. Dear Dr. Nassar,

could words send a shiver through a sniper's finger?
Will tears buy a bandage? You stopped counting
(you wrote today) your injured, some of whom are

lying out there still ...
Is it any comfort to know that the tanks murdering
in my name are digging a grave for my people as well?

Translated by Peter Cole

The Story of the Arab Who Died in the Fire / Dahlia Ravikovitch

When the fire seized his body, it didn't happen by slow degrees.
No burst of heat to begin with,
no stifling billow of smoke
no prospect of a room next door where one could escape.
The fire took him all at once,
such a thing hath not its likeness,
it peeled away his clothing
seized upon his flesh,
the first casualties were the nerves in the skin
then the hair fell prey to the fire,
God, they're burning us, he screamed,
that's all he could manage in self-defense.
The flesh was blazing along with the planks of the shed
which sustained the fire in the primary phase.
By that point his mental faculties were gone,
the firebrand of the flesh
paralyzed any sense of a future,
the memories of his family
the links to his childhood.
He was shrieking, no longer constrained by reason,
by now all the bonds of family were broken,
he did not seek vengeance, redemption, the dawn of a new day.

All he wanted was to stop burning
but his own body kept feeding the blaze
as if he were bound and laid on the altar
though he wasn't thinking about that, either.
He went on burning by the sheer force of his body,
flesh and fat and sinews.
And he kept on burning.
From his throat issued inhuman voices
since many human functions had already ceased
except for the pain transmitted in electrical pulses
along neural pathways to pain receptors in the brain.
All of this lasted no more than a single day.
And it's a good thing he breathed his last when he did
because he deserved to rest.

Translated by Chana Bloch and Chana Kronfeld

The Observing Heart / Asher Reich

"Only his voice can I still remember!"
the bereaved father's whisper burns into me. Impassively,
like a dead spirit, he lights for himself daily

a path to the cemetery. The observing heart knows:
Here the sons die before the fathers.
Here where it is thick with rot. The fruit dies
before the tree (planted in his yard on the boy's birth).

I see a graveyard: its facade is as luminous as ruin.
Our death's crowning glory. Here is the chosen place
where sons die before fathers. In the rot,
exploits of a land are woven in insolent silence:
the naiveté, the lies, and everything that death swallows up.

Translated by Rachel Tzvia Back

Kaddish / Yitzhak Laor

Every day is a day
of remembrance for someone
who died. He who has
a grave and he who has
nowhere to cry

He who has mourners, he who
doesn't, she who has
truth, she who
doesn't, he whom others
have built on top
of his dead and he may not
dig, and he who destroys
the house of the dead

Every day is a day of remembrance.
Every day someone dies
is killed in the name
of a forgotten dead, every
day someone is forgotten, every
day someone retreats into the air
without an epitaph: unfathomable Land
layer upon layer, if only all your slain
were remembered, if only all
were forgotten

Translated by Gabriel Levin

from And Who Will Remember the Rememberers? / Yehuda Amichai

3.

What is the correct way to stand at a memorial ceremony?
Erect or stooped, pulled taut as a tent or in the slumped posture
of mourning, head bowed like the guilty or held high
in a collective protest against death,
eyes gaping frozen like the eyes of the dead
or shut tight, to see stars inside?
And what is the best time for remembering? At noon
when shadows are hidden beneath our feet, or at twilight
when shadows lengthen like longings
that have no beginning, no end, like God?

4.

And what should our lament be? David's lament over Saul and Jonathan:
"Swifter than eagles, stronger than lions," that is what our lament should be.

Had they really been swifter than eagles
they would have soared high above war
and would not have been hurt. From down here, we would have seen them
and said: "There go the eagles! There is my son, my husband, my brother."

And had they really been stronger than lions
they would have stayed like lions, not died like human beings.
They would have eaten out of our hands,
we would have stroked their golden manes,
we would have tamed them in our homes, with love:
My son, my husband, my brother, my husband, my son.

Translated by Chana Bloch and Chana Kronfeld

IV

The Hands—
They Were the Hands of Soldiers

Soldiers / Rami Saari

What's left behind us, what do we leave behind?
Lands of long mourning
filled with quiet olives,
the shadow of mosques on the horizon, smoky skies.
Along the remote paths
wrecked by bombs
an exhausted convoy shuffles: tools of destruction
and then the young men. We don't remember
the beautiful songs we once knew by heart.
In the conflicted past
blue shirts and red flags turned into one fabric
of lies. From the hill
where we stood, you can see
the secrets of destruction, sometimes
we still wonder why we insisted on keeping
the human image we've lost.

Translated by Lisa Katz

Toy Soldiers / Aharon Shabtai

And why didn't you bring flowers
a truck loaded down with bouquets
for the impoverished children of Rafi'ah?
Or sacks of cheap sweaters for the mothers
or Chinese lighters for the fathers?
And why didn't you waken them
with a bundle of umbrellas and raincoats?
Or a jeep full of fireworks to spread, for a moment,
a canopy of splendor over the puddles?
Haven't you read Andersen's "The Flying Trunk"?
You could have used the bulldozer's maw
to shovel bread to the doors of the houses.
To deposit cartons of milk in secret.
Don't you know how to surprise?
Don't your brains contain even an ounce of imagination?
You could easily have used the cover
of darkness to build a playground in silence,
or put back the electric poles in the alleys
or stock the clinic with drugs!
Haven't you heard of Louis Pasteur?
What muck have you filled your heads with,
that you came by night in the driving rain
to tear down seventy miserable shanties
and toss seven hundred people—
women and children—into the mud?
Idiotic soldiers of lead,
was your father a knife
that only knows how to chop?
Or your mother a pair of scissors
that only knows how to sever?

Translated by Peter Cole

The Letters' Rebellion / Zvi Atzmon

Fishing boats—
dark moles bobbing up and down,
kept away from the beach until dawn.
The moon's circle is a white patch
on the sea's heart, ECG.
The padded metal helmet leaves little room
for imagination.
From the guava orchards, the dull smell
of surrender.
Wind-tears in the open jeep at the security fence.
Smoke from the huts.
Two camels.
A bare-legged old man pulls in a net.
R.C. is for Radio Contact, and that's an order,
a curfew is a curfew.
R.C. is for Refugee Camp, it's about time you know this.
Sign here, damn it,
N.S.B. stands for Non-Standard Baton—
any handle of a shovel—efficient, don't worry—
give me your military number, *ya-habibi*, and signature too.
Rubber is rubber.
Plastic is plastic.
A tire is for burning.
Gas is for tears.
R.D. is for Reserve Duty.
And a soldier is a soldier.
M.O.O.N. is moon.
W.H.I.T.E. is white.
And T.H.A.T.'s that.
Terror. Terrible.

Translated by Rachel Tzvia Back

Poem for Muhammad / Admiel Kosman

Muhammad, oh Muhammad, are you still awake?
The soldiers are sleeping while the wind blows
over the curled-up village, and I am the messenger
or watchman.

Something like that.

Strange: can a blind man be a watchman?
Someone up there needs to check.
Perhaps there's been an oversight.
Perhaps my file was switched with someone else's?

The wind blows
over the curled-up village, and I am the messenger
or watchman.

Something like that.

Ridiculous. After all I've been duly appointed as a representative
of my party, and also guard, soldier on horseback, policeman,
faithful envoy, the one and only, oh oh, watch out, my Mohammed,
don't tell them my secret.
And don't wake them up.

The wind blows
over the curled-up village, and I am the messenger
or watchman.

Something like that.

Who knows? Listen
and you'll hear me:
if tomorrow by mistake you awaken
those dead-and-buried in the village ground,
digging in yesterday's sands, everything
inside will crumble and be gone.

The wind blows
over the curled-up village, and I am the messenger
or watchman.

Something like that.

Translated by Lisa Katz

Calf / Yitzhak Laor

Under the moon cold as a wet bench in a cordoned-off city
during a curfew, we return on a different path as if from the fresh
mound of a grave (Dona Dona) pushing a handcuffed detainee
forward, dragging an informant from behind (Dona Dona),
Jewish history (Dona
Dona) is the voice and the hands—the sweating hands
of the soldiers, their boots, and the rifles stinking
of oil. In the canteen the sentry and the officer were
arm wrestling, the canteen attendant also wanted to, but they ignored him
(because he was a private and not because he was
Moroccan, Dona Dona etc.)*

*A word from the poet: I have no
choice. Even if all is produced
by the regime—the history
of poetry, as well as the boundaries
of speech—I have no choice
but to resist.

Translated by Gabriel Levin

[The platoon left] / Tsvika Szternfeld

The platoon left.
The Border Patrol retreated.
Radio silence.
Silence all around us.
The street is empty.
A young father (child in his arms)
rushes to the hospital.
His wife, with worried expression, right behind him.
The boy is bleeding from his mouth.
Thank God—
there are injuries which have nothing to do with us.
"And the stride,"
I say to Y.S.,
"there is no mistaking the stride—
the hurried stride of a worried father
with a child in his arms."

Translated by Rachel Tzvia Back

Transparent / Ronny Someck

Tayyib studies literature at Tel-Aviv University.
He has a backpack with a grammar book and a composition
about Mahmoud Darwish.
The backpack is transparent because this summer
with any other bag,
in the X-ray eyes of all policemen, he is marked
as hiding a bomb.
"Even this," his father says, "*inshallah*,
will soon come out in the wash," and hangs on
the timeline clothes from which a stain
of shame has been rinsed. But
life has to go to the market, and he goes with it
to buy olives in vernacular Arabic and write
poems about them in literary Arabic.
Meanwhile, Tayyib is entirely exposed to view. The taut skin
on his arms does not hide the knots of muscle,
the flexible cartilage in the space between the bones
and the blood vessels in which
the swimmer of despair can crawl drunken
to the shore where the lifeguards have hung
a black flag.

Translated by Vivian Eden

There Is a God / Amir Or

Come, come here, come over here, boy.
Stand straight when I'm talking to you.
Papers.
Ahh.
Tell me, you piece of shit, when
did your parents fuck up and make you?

He was nineteen and a half
smiled all the time and wore a blazer.
El-Ghazali St., Shua'fat.
A student of economics or something.
A clear case.
I kneed him
in the balls.

He doubled over and started to vomit.
I gave him another
in the face.
Then another
with the rifle butt.
I lit a cigarette.
And the radio.
He lay in the bushes shaking:
my barrel rose up on its own.

I reported on the wireless.
An exact shot, straight to the cross-seams.
1–0.

Translated by Rachel Tzvia Back

Execution / Gilad Meiri

Our routine patrol identified a suspicious
figure in an abandoned house we surprised
him (or maybe it was her)
and he was caught after a short debriefing
we understood this was a wanted man or actually
a woman (it's hard to tell these days) so
we had to execute him or
her and you must understand we
couldn't take prisoners but
because of what happened to Lorca you know
we received instructions to wait until
there was clearance from headquarters and believe me
or don't in the end we shot him or
her with clearance and all but
later it turned out there was a computer
or human
error and we shot this suspicious
figure for no reason but
because it was a mistake he or
she didn't die or is still not
officially
dead
this kind of thing
happened every day
back then was in the newspapers but
only today
can we talk about it.

Translated by Rachel Tzvia Back

One Minute / Shai Dotan

Just one minute. I want
to scream. I shot him. He advanced
with a suspicious face. Who knew his pockets
were empty, his bag full of clothes.

Perhaps he didn't have a work permit,
or once stole across the border. Maybe he didn't hear
my hands shouting, the blood
pounding in the chest, knocking on my temples.

Sometimes he wakes in my sleep,
hard as lead, empty as the wind,
and says to me: My killer,
I never knew
you were one of them.

Translated by Rachel Tzvia Back

The Hands—They Were the Hands of Soldiers   /   65

V

And If the Dead Is a Child, Will Someone Gather Him Up?

To a Pilot / Aharon Shabtai

When next you circle
in your chopper
over Jenin,
pilot, remember the children
and old women
in the homes at which you fire.
Spread a layer
of chocolate across your missile,
and do your best to be precise—
so their souvenir will be sweet
when the walls start to fall.

Translated by Peter Cole

I Protest / Aryeh Sivan

A comment on the attached photo

I wipe the dust off my books
with a small t-shirt, an old t-shirt
which was once my son's. We have
more dust this summer than last,
and its composition is different too:
mixed in it are pieces of plaster and paint
maybe from the houses that were blown up. In any case
after an hour or so of dusting, stripes
of many shades
appear on the garment. Normally
I would think of Joseph
the gifted and beautiful boy, the wise boy who knew how
to extricate himself so tactfully
from every trouble that befell his family, the boy who dreamt
of wheat stacks, the boy who went to Shechem
to tend his sheep. But today
I can't get out of my mind
the picture of a different beautiful boy
from Shechem: Here he is before you, lying motionless,
and the hole in his chest is not
from the teeth of a wild beast.

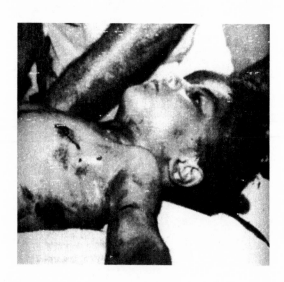

Coke and Jeans / Yosef Ozer

The same week Jews read in the synagogue
the section in the Bible about
Sarah's banishment of Hagar and Ishmael,
seven-year-old Ali Jawarish was wounded
by a plastic-tipped bullet
that penetrated straight through to his brain.
Ali Jawarish became a vegetable.
He lay dying in an Israeli hospital for two whole days,
and the Angel of Death who arrived
did not show the well to Ali's mother.

The same week Jews read in the synagogue
the section in the Bible about
the binding of Isaac,
Ali Jawarish was divided into several parts—
one 15-year-old boy received Ali's liver and lungs.
The boy's mother told the media
that her son sat up in bed and asked for
a Coke and a pair of jeans.
Ali's father said that they would also donate his son's organs
to a Jew (yesterday
a Jewish soldier was divided up
among a number of Arabs).

This insane poem is begging to be written.

Perhaps in this way, slowly and delicately
we will carry out a population transfer:
Palestinians will receive the organs of Jews
and Jews the organs of Palestinians

and Sarah our Matriarch
and Hagar their Matriarch
will be oh so pleased with their lot,
and we will all drink Cokes and wear jeans.

Translated by Mark Elliott Shapiro

[Stripes of light on the wall] / Maya Bejerano

Stripes of light on the wall,
color of the sun, invisible letters
in the lines which haven't yet found for themselves shape or meaning,
an image of presence—
the terrorist's blood mixing with the blood of those he hated—
we within a new and terrifying brew.
So
hollowed-out children hide behind a costume facade
borrowed for a moment
until their insides, shocked sober, bid it farewell—
a new life-lesson engraved on them:
play and pleasure's pendulum is designed to swing down,
tiring, it betrays them—
and how will they return to the festivities?
To that same colorful carrousel, its straps cut loose,
its joyous riders tossed into the abyss?

They know
yes they know
for they have the wisdom of children.

(Purim, March 1996, Tel-Aviv)

Translated by Rachel Tzvia Back

Nur / Mei-Tal Nadler

In the marketplace they are still clearing away the carnage. Smoke
is welded to car skeletons, piles of cabbage, onions,
the smells of spices and parsley
trapped in the scorched flesh.

At noon, fire reigned here. A monastery's silver turrets paled.
Rage twisted through the alleys. Bursting forth all at once. Round and whole
like a universe unto itself. Consuming the densest and noisiest things,
indiscriminately.

In the yard someone tied the four wheels of a baby carriage
to a white plastic chair, for the boy Nur.
But what lies between you and me, Nur? Not even a wadi
of cabbage fields, where your two dead brothers
entangled in the sun, slip away.

At night, time and memory become true enemies.
Beyond the paralyzed anger, the chains of houses—
a giant's necklace in a shining village.
And who will pay, Nur?
Will the village pay? No.
The wadi? No.
Will the earth pay? No, the earth won't pay.

The earth on which all your tall fears will walk.

Translated by Rachel Tzvia Back

Author's Note: In August 2002, the children of Khaled and Hanan Ismail from the
village of Irtas went to shop in the Dehayshe market. In the explosion that ensued, Nidal
(thirteen) and Abed (twelve) were killed. Nur Ismail (fifteen) lost both his legs. No Israeli
or Palestinian organization ever took responsibility for the incident.

October 2000 / Oreet Meital

Dedicated to Muhammed Al-Dura
who was killed in his father's arms,
and to his father, Gamal

1.

And he who dies, does he really reach out with empty hands?
Abandoned to his spirit, does he gather into the dusty land,
unto his fathers, his limbs trembling?

His nostrils, will they ever again pick up the scent of flowers
spreading deep, darker and more intoxicating
in the earth than in the air?

For his sake, will a candle burn bright? When his soul leaves
his body, becomes light? Transfigured in another?
A tree? A stone? In a tiger?

And if he is a child, is there someone who will gather him up with tender grace?
Weeping with him for the pain of his bullet-riddled hands which could not
                                                                    protect his face?
Will he taste of the Leviathan's meat?
Will he hover for a moment
between here and there?

And if he is old, will he reach the gate? The light?
Will he strip down to his soul as in a holy place and rid
himself of all these questions and of the others too?

2.

And after some days, many days
will he let us lead him astray
for a split second
to the séance
where his cross-armed kin
bow their heads before the empty space
begging forgiveness.

After many days
will there be one among them who stays open-eyed

who reaches out for him
and caresses him
and with his spirit failing him

doesn't blow the dust from his eyes
and doesn't say that with him gone,
even with him gone, everything continues as it was

and here, in the darkness, if we breathe in anything
it is forgetting.

Translated by Rachel Tzvia Back

The Love of Truth / Yitzhak Laor

Because of the love of truth, the root of memory, I'm saving for you, my son,
your first toy, and the first tooth that fell out, a shining diamond
your fear over the wobbly tooth, because of the love of truth, the name
of the midwife, Zemira, who showed you to me for the first time, and the
name of Dr. Boaz, from the preemies ward, who saved your life and
watched over it like a bluish flower (and over the lives of thousands of
Jewish and Arab babies) and the video clip from the news on which the boy
Muhammad al-Dura from Gaza is begging for his life, before shot in his
father's arms, who is begging for his son's life and the soldiers can't restrain
themselves, because at home it is forbidden to kill children in their fathers'
arms, or in the doctor's waiting room, or on the bus traveling at dusk from
the market back to their neighborhood, I'm saving it for you my son,
so you can watch it again and again, part of your childhood memories,
for the sake of truth, which is the root of memory,
the place to distinguish good from bad, to know whom to fear and whom to
forgive, and to whom to extend a soft hand, keep your hands soft my son (and
I've destroyed the photos of me in uniform, you should know)

The sniper said (with a tone of regret)
what will I do when my army stint ends?

Translated by Rachel Tzvia Back

The Man Who Apparently Caused the Death of Hilmi Shusha / Dan Daor

> A blessing on him who seizes your babies
> and dashes them against the rocks.
> —Psalms 137:9

The man who apparently caused the death of Hilmi Shusha
did not shoot him in cold blood, make no mistake,
for he is the merciful son of merciful fathers and as far as we know
he only beat him, and the boy is dead.

He is not the manly Baruch Goldstein,
he too was a Jew of morals, make no mistake,
and as far as we know he did not murder crowds,
he only beat up one ten-year-old boy, indeed no longer a baby,
beat him, and the boy is dead.

He did not desecrate the body, as far as we know,
neither did he say Happy Holidays over the blood,
because he is not a sadist, neither is he Hanan Porat, make no mistake,
he only beat up Hilmi Shusha,
beat him, and the boy is dead.

He did not murder and inherit, as far as we know,
because he is not Achav, may the dogs lap up his blood,
he is only a Jewish security officer, make no mistake,
who beat up a boy, and the boy is dead.

Translated by Rachel Tzvia Back

The Day of Blood / Sharron Hass

For Hilmi Shusha

1.
We wanted to drop our hearts
off the porch; we knew the hearts of the old people
would reach the ground first, then the middle-aged ones,
and the children's last. But the bad man's smile
stretched out above us, and in his presence we didn't dare compete with
 suffering.
We closed the shutters. All night we heard him laughing
outside the house, slowly, patiently,
as one struck so hard on the mouth by angels
that his body forgot how to store its humanity
and eluded the growing weight of pain.
We didn't dare step outside. We pretended we forgot
where we put our hearts,
red, humiliated, unable to cover their own nakedness.

2.
I hardly know your name, but
I have seen a green flower in frost
cover your face in victory.
Before life caught up with you
the bad man was there, the one with no need
for animals, for he has the neighbor's children.

3.
Night begins to stride, I follow
silently. When he bends
over the child's mouth, the hart's ears freeze.
My fear and the most anxious of animals
hear nothing. The child refuses to say
to whom he belongs. Only night waits
 to strike.

4.

A child stands at the doorway. No. Not exactly
the doorway. A child frozen
        on the verge of consciousness, the arm of a chair
the eye of a needle. I see, not with my eyes, but
with the fourth, the fifth eye
the lidless one, thrust in the back,
seeing those who stand and do not cross the threshold.
You don't want to leave and I don't want you to go.

Through me you see a tree hung in the window,
and the sun leaps onto the blue backs of the birds
        through me you see
        a dead little girl
appearing suddenly in the public park,
her mouth torn out and thrown into a hedge
and night, still half-hidden in the earth,
gripping her naked body,
climbing on her ankles, leaving red
stripes on her stomach.

I was smuggled away like a precious doll wrapped in rags
        from the land of one God to the land of idols,
        a large and beautiful silence galloped alongside me—
it took you on its back
        when you were flung aside, nauseous, like a bitter green fruit,
to ride far away from the day of blood.

You are moving toward me now, your arms blue with the effort,
to grab my hair—look I am turning
toward you and all my years rebel, look a naked girl rises
from the hedges, look I present you with the body I didn't know
was mine, with which I could not stop,
then as now,
the death of another,
which is also mine.

Translated by Lisa Katz

A Mother Is Walking Around / Dahlia Ravikovitch

A mother is walking around with a dead child in her belly.
This child hasn't been born yet.
On the day of his birth, the dead child will be born
head first, then back and buttocks
and he won't wave his arms about
or cry his first cry
and they won't tap his bottom
or put drops in his eyes
and they won't swaddle him
after washing his body.
He'll be nothing like a living child.
And his mother won't be calm and proud after giving birth
she also won't be worried about his future,
she won't ask herself how will she support him
and does she have enough milk
and enough clothes
and how will she fit another cradle into the room.
This child is wholly righteous,
unmade ere he was ever made.
And he'll have his own little grave at the edge of the cemetery
and a little memorial day
and very little to remember him by.
This is the history of the child
who was killed in his mother's belly
in the month of January 1988,
for reasons relating to national security.

Translated by Rachel Tzvia Back

Landscape with Fear in the Eye / Yitzhak Laor

Somewhere at the edge where the eye sees no fear
a mother runs barefoot through the hills in search of her son
between roadblocks she doesn't hear the centurions sneering
at her, she doesn't care (anyway they're talking about soccer) just
bring her son back home, his entire life is still before him. Within
the wasteland, nature mute, almost colorless
nothing is heard, and pain isn't seen because there is no pain
in a place where the ear cannot hear a sigh, in a place where the ear
trusts only truth, detecting the stutter of the liar at the roadblock—
"Truth is a signifier without a signified," says the seasoned interrogator
to his wife at the end of the day, dead tired, he'll take a vacation, he'll pack
a novel maybe they'll be fruitful and multiply in the hotel,
in the evening after they feast
(Rabbi Eliezer said: "Anyone who isn't engaged in procreation—
it is as though he is spilling blood").

In a place where the eye doesn't see olive trees if they aren't its own, where
the ear is annoyed by the laughter of children if it doesn't understand
their language, where the eye doesn't see its blindness, the ear doesn't hear
its deafness, we thrust words into the throat of the victim so he won't be
a victim, in the name of the Jewish nation, dreaming always of Jerusalem,
a dunam here and a dunam there another dunam here and another dunam
there. O fields of the valley, let us spread out.

And the mother is standing at ravine's edge, weeping, she's found her son, he's
alive, she wants to call out in joy, hesitates, embarrassed (it's an hour after
burying her sister's son) precisely now when she sees her son alive
under his secret tree, she remembers how fragile her home is, how
she didn't think of this while running (at night it's forbidden to go out, only
they come in the dark, break down the doors, rip off the blankets, running
wherever they want, we're Arabs, they're soldiers in Arab disguise) and
"the valley is a dream"

Translated by Gabriel Levin

The Target / Tal Nitzan

They closed their non-aiming eye
and watched the target
and chose an aiming point
and brought the edge of the blade
to the notch of the rear sight
with all the gunsights upright
and leaving a white thread
they fired.
But missed.
They did manage to kill Muhammad El-Hayk, 24,
and severely wound his father Abdalla, 64,
all "as necessary and according to procedures,"
but missed Maisun El-Hayk,
only slightly wounding her
in spite of her big belly
that happened to be a perfect aiming point
(but hadn't they made her undress at the roadblock before
to ensure the belly was a belly indeed
and the labor pains—labor pains
before it occurred to them
to proceed with
"suspect arrest-procedure"?)
and also failed to hit
her fetus daughter
and send her to heaven
before she came into this world
—must have overlooked that white thread—
but did manage to inseparably seam
her birth day to her father's burial day
and reinforce the promise
"In sorrow thou shalt bring forth children"
—there has been no greater sorrow!—
as the shooting ceased
and Maisun called out for Muhammad
and the terror or the excruciating pain
twisted her voice
("Breathe slowly and deeply,
find the most comfy position,
think of something nice and pleasant,

ask your partner to dim the lights,
play your favorite music,
gently massage your lower back")
and he, suddenly, stopped answering,
for if you haven't seen Maisun's photo,
her hands quivering over her daughter,
pink, calm, innocent
the way newborn babies are
—but wasn't she lucky
to have given birth to her in a hospital bed
rather than crouching like her sisters before her
like an animal in front of the soldiers
and then stumbling ten kilometers,
walking and bleeding,
carrying the dead infant as an offering—
whoever hasn't opened a non-aiming eye
to look into Maisun El-Hayk's face,
has never seen what it means
to bring forth children in sorrow.

Translated by Tal Nitzan, with Vivian Eden

VI

He Who Demolishes
A Person's Home

Retinal Tear / Dvora Amir

> All people are the same in their nakedness, as are
> houses when they become heaps of rubble.*

One could sense there the atmosphere of just before a terrible act.
A heavy engine inserted a blast into the earth.
Into my widened pupils a house collapsed,
crumbled, landing in the eye's depths.
A puzzle of frozen dryness, as on the bottom of a dying lake,
was etched into my eyes. "Retinal tear," you said,
and I know there are some sights for which there is no repair:
an armless old man flapping his empty sleeves toward his face,
a girl looking for her notebook in the ruins.
And later, the curses of women who were torn from the walls of their house
drilled into my eye-socket, and I told myself,
whoever scars a person's home—in the end his eyes will be scarred,
whoever demolishes a person's home—in the end his soul will be demolished.

Beit Sahour

Translated by Rachel Tzvia Back

*Written by Olga Friedberg, niece of Boris Pasternak, on the ruins of Leningrad under siege.

Written and Signed / Aryeh Sivan

I meant to write: with his eye
that was rooted out by a rubber bullet
he sees clearly every point in the village
from which he was uprooted: the prickly sabra bushes
beyond the stone fences,
the motherly fig tree and the olive, its trunk
gnarled like his grandfather's face.
He will pass on these sights
to his firstborn son and to his other
surviving children
in order to nail them, with the thorns of the sabra,
to their land.

I meant to write that. I didn't.
Between intention and execution
a shadow fell.
Not the shadows of villages,
but the shadows of people
moving toward me, carrying
what looks like documents
folded and creased:
promissory notes
which were buried in the ruins.
They are holding them out to me
to sign.

Translated by Rachel Tzvia Back

Fifteen Minutes to *Khurban Ha'Bayit* / Yoram Levy Porat

A Mediterranean song
from "The Jews' Opera"

Fifteen minutes to *khurban ha'bayit*
fifteen minutes is a long time.
A house painted on a white page
chimney of galvanized tin
shutters a hideous blue.
Damn it, from where did they bring such terrible taste.

Fifteen minutes to *khurban ha'bayit*
fifteen minutes is a long time.
Pots, pans,
chimney of galvanized tin
blankets, pillows, old bedspread,
an embroidered silk bird
panteth after the water brooks.

Fifteen minutes to *khurban ha'bayit*
fifteen minutes is a long time.
Dresses, jewelry,
galvanized tin chimney,
china set, spoons, old English kettle,
an embroidered silk bird
panteth after the water brooks.

Fifteen minutes to *khurban ha'bayit*
fifteen minutes is a long time.
Strings, buttons,
galvanized tin chimney,
sheets, vases, dry spices,
pictures of the sea
a galvanized tin chimney,
stove, phone from the mandate days,
toilet, army surplus plates,
cutlery, mats, paper dolls,
records, Umm Kulthum
a dictionary of spoken Hebrew,
an embroidered silk bird
panteth after the water brooks.

Fifteen minutes to *khurban ha'bayit*
fifteen minutes is a long time.
A house painted on a white page
a chimney of galvanized tin
shutters of hideous blue.
Damn it, from where did they bring this terrible taste.

An embroidered silk bird
panteth after the water brooks.
Fifteen minutes to the house demolition
fifteen minutes is a long time.

Translated by Rachel Tzvia Back

Author's Note: The Hebrew phrase *khurban ha'bayit*—which literally means "destruction of the house"—refers to the destruction of the First Temple (586 BCE) and the Second Temple (70 CE) in Jerusalem. The *khurban* evokes the greatest of calamities that befell the Jews, as embodied in these destructions and the resulting exile.

The Fence / Aharon Shabtai

The fence—
winding for miles
between the orchards
like a pickpocket's hand—
is set deep in the mind,
and so the face
shrivels as though
between pincers
to the size of a piece
of note-paper.
Where, O face,
is your Africa now?
Where are the birds
of being human?
Give me at least
a thousand dunams
of average justice
and I'll find you a face
that isn't simply equipment
for searching out and chewing.

It isn't the hand of God that opens
and locks a gate
before a woman or mule with scars—
but the stupid soldier in a scarecrow's fatigues.
The fence is education—
soup kitchens
with bowls of ignorance.
And the fence is speech,
the Hebrew language,
rolling around like the wash
with which a decent person
wouldn't wipe his nose.
And the fence is rows of homes,
in which the vile man
has settled himself on a throne
and rumbles from the screen
to drown out the cries of the beaten
bubbling up from the tiles and floors.
And the fence is economics—

transporting a mother toward penury,
carting the letter containing
an order for eviction
toward the kitchen table
and the high-school student who sets
his book-bag down and shoots himself.

I open the refrigerator door
and see a weeping roll,
see a piece of bleeding cheese,
a radish forced to sprout
by shocks from wires
and blows from fists.
The meat on its plate
tells of placentas
cast aside by roadblocks.

I went to a village
where the hens lay
eggs of stone,
where the bread is baked
from ground homes,
and the eyes of people
peer out from behind their teeth.
Where only the mouse knows freedom.

I lift my eyes to the hills
and what do I see?
Cube after cube of evil,
clear-cut evil, spelled out
in the square letters of Scripture
with marks for cantillation:
word adheres to word
by means of iniquity's mortar.
The foundations cling to plunder,
the walls to pillars of dispossession,
the doors are planks of oppression,
and, cut into panes of malice,
the windows hang
by thievery's hinges,
as rooftops curse the sky.

Translated by Peter Cole

Curfew, Variation #5 / Diti Ronen

Time hovers here above a single body, then a second,
sun, cloud, moon, blockaded routine. How does pain mend?
A snatched breath, a short break between dark and light, a forced doze,
a sudden drop of the head, flashes flickering here, and later there.

The morning rain shames the trees and me—our disgrace, heavy and wet, is dragged
earthward. The bed is an island dug by length and breadth in an endless search
for the body's hollow and heat. I curl up, contract into almost nothing, but pain
has its own rules—restriction of movement and absence of free passage
     entrench the sinking, the deep fog.

At night, below the surface, a vast river of consciousness bursts forth, pushing
forward, forging its own course. Roadblocks are temporary obstacles, as are
the mud-drenched detours and feet—obedient as they may be—falter,
     sometimes from fear.

Outside it's Friday. The aroma of the neighbor's *mansaf* lingers in the laundry shed.
I try to understand what day it is inside, but the light is the same darkness. Soon
the flickering will end, and the fire and dark flashes will vanish, into
     the quiet of mending.

Translated by Rachel Tzvia Back

from **The Olive / Avner Treinin**

In the olive grove of Ein-Kerem, the Arab plough
strikes a boulder, pounds in my head. Shh, shh, refugee,
lest you awaken the village in Jewish Jerusalem.

After independence it was abandoned property,
and he, abandoned without property.
Wild branch and rotten fruit on the olive trees
cry out to him to hear and reach

up to pick the fruit. A guard (what is there to guard?)
apprehends him, the police take
fingerprints, a file is then opened for the criminal,
the refugee from Kerem-Navot.

Translated by Rachel Tzvia Back

There Is No One Here / Rachel Dana

The Mozart playing against the window-panes of the closed car
does not break the silence of Armon Ha'Natziv, six before
the day awakens, the Dome of the Rock is not glistening in the sun
the few fir trees saved from Christmas cutting do not hide
the soldiers waiting to stop the traffic.
There is no one here. There is no one here

to come and tell me the olive tree will bloom in good time
and the rain will paint purple the carpets of rosemary
and the people will still return to roll grape leaves
and the fig will not spill its seed in vain
and the wind now displacing the fog
with thick smoke rising from the blown-up house in A-Tur
will blow away all the bad thoughts of the children
who have learned only the history of the last 36 years

Translated by Rachel Tzvia Back

From the Songs of *Tu B'Shevat*—The Festival of Tree Planting / Avner Treinin

(an adaptation of children's songs)

From hills, valleys, and rain-pools,
why have you come here to rule?

We'll crush and we'll crush,
expose roots and underbrush
of almond and olive.

From village, town, and farmland,
what do you plan here to plant?

We'll strike rock and ground,
dig holes all around,
on the hills and the plains
to plant corpses in graves.

Translated by Rachel Tzvia Back

Olive Tree / Agi Mishol

shafted, stuck among three coconut palms
in a layer of gravel from the Home Depot
in the middle of a junction turned overnight
into a square.

Motorists hurrying home
see it perhaps
through clay pots tilting over,
but they have no time for the twisted story
that rises from its trunk or the flat top of the tree,
trimmed with a building contractor's sense of humor.

Nor can they fathom their roots groping
in foreign soil
clutching mother earth
like provisions from home
since the soldiers cut them down.

The olives, offered and unwanted, blacken
my face
and no miniature roses will divert my heart
from the shame.

Translated by Lisa Katz

[You've changed your name] / Gil Engelstein

You've changed your name, Jason.
You've left the slough to rot in the field.
Maybe you thought your past
would disintegrate together with it,
become fertilizer,
in heaps far from the heart.
Zionism created for you a new name.
You are no longer a Jewish American Prince—
you are Ilan, a tree.
Groping for your roots in the land of Palestine,
as in a desperate desire to change, to become
an ancient olive covered in dust, or
a fig heavy with juice.

When I see you strutting in your green uniform,
you're lustily fingering the weapon
you were given,
excited like a teenage boy
who has discovered for the first time
the flushed swelling in his pants. Deaf
to the wind's moaning in the olive branches, deaf
to the silent wisdom of the fig,
you salute the pine trees,
planted in rows in the military cemetery,
as black as frozen screams.

Jason Jason Jason,
names are just
a passing comfort.

The silence between us has made us
strangers.
Only your fleeting gaze recalls for me
the cold and hurried winter touch
of the intefada's beginning,
when you would crawl into my bed, stripped bare,
wet, trembling beyond touch,
and speaking truth.

The strings of silence are being stretched between us,
lengthening daily.
When you break free of the cocoon of forgetting
in which you have wrapped yourself,
the strings will halt your flight
and wound your wings,
>   and I won't be there anymore
>   to patch them up
>   kiss
>   by kiss.

Translated by Rachel Tzvia Back

VII

Sing for Us
from the Songs of Zion

Our Captors Required of Us a Song / Dahlia Ravikovitch

> How shall we sing a song of Zion
> when we've not even begun to listen?
> —Lea Goldberg

Sing for us from the songs of Zion
which will ascend to a deaf ear.
Sing intimate songs
that the soul shies away from singing
beyond the inner circle
within the house.
Hasten and sing for us a new song—
we'll pull the song from your throats with pliers.
What is the Holy Ark's curtain and the Temple
to you?
We have a wild need to cause pain
and to torture.
For what are we without your agony?
A broken vessel.
The hatred in your throats is also a broken vessel.
Look at us:
we have hung your lyres
far away
on the willows.
Now you must carve a path with cracked voices
like the donkey ascending the cliffs of Tyre
or like the bull's deep lowing
this way and that.

Translated by Rachel Tzvia Back

To the Muses / Agi Mishol

Forgive me, O eternal ones,
for disturbing you with our history
repeating itself

exactly the way the smart wildflowers return,
and the purple loosestrife spreads over my lawn,
but suddenly it's hard to be gratified by beauty
whose entire aim is itself.

Heavenly ones, floating among gauze scarves,
ivory combs in your golden hair,
what do you have in common with the old women in the Kandahar hills
gathering crab grass to feed the swollen-bellied children,
or with the women bending over the rubble in Rafah—
like poisonous black mushrooms rising from the ruins.

How well I know the language of your wildflowers.
I won't trouble you to sneak away with me
in the middle of the night
to pet laboratory monkeys,
or plant compassion in the heart of the farmer
burning the horns off a calf's skull.

But don't turn my eyes today
toward the pink edge of the cloud castle,
don't signal the triumph of eternity
in the birds' V.

Translated by Lisa Katz

Searching the Land / Rami Saari

The poem isn't served meat and fruit
on a silver platter at night,
and by day its mouth does not long
for a golden spoon or communion wafers.
Lost, it wanders the roads of Beit Jala,
sways like a drunk through the streets of Bethlehem,
seeking you along the way in vain,
searching for your shadow's shadow in the shrubs.

Close to the breast, the soul sits
curled up like a boy in a sleeping bag,
dry as a flower bulb buried in the middle of the throat.
Then the poem feels it can't go on any longer
wandering towards the refugee camp,
toward the fugitives' cradle
in the Promised Land's heavy summer,
on the path to disaster.

Translated by Lisa Katz

Pro & Con / Meir Wieseltier

I can't stand political poetry: that civil or prophetic posturing
(Why should a citizen speak in broken lines?)
or the irony of paper fighter planes facing steel and bulletproof glass
    and the elephant stampede
of the electorate and the elected.
It's disgusting, the glory of bamboo arrows versus dive-bombers
or, just as bad, that prophetic stance:
ventriloquism in the name of History, the facile analogies, truisms,
master plans for redemption. Quiet!
Let's have some quiet here—
let the poet turn inward, let him study his navel,
dream of his father and mother,
or draw the pigeons on the neighbor's roof—
a street in the city, a house on the street,
a room inside the house, an orange peel on the table
slowly
drying.

Just not that spectacle:
someone on edge picks up the morning paper,
listens to news on the hour, follows
the TV broadcasts—and by late evening is ready to hold forth
(render unto the politician what belongs to Caesar, and unto the journalist
    what belongs to the eunuch).
Just not that spectacle. And above all,
quiet. Quiet, I say.
Let there be quiet here.

But sometimes I can't control myself, and like a pervert
I sneak up on the wax figures' display.
Here they are, lined up in a row, those gawky masks in charge
of deciding our fate in these times.
They are posed with the postures of men who get things done,
they sit skewed by the weight of responsibility,
smiling their smiles almost like humans
or earnestly staring with molded expressions.

And I emerge into the coolness of lampposts,
a street, locked shops,
look at a flicker in the glass.

Light and free. Cold and hot.
Here and not.
Blood and rot. Snot.
I say, snot-shot.

Translated by Shirley Kaufman

The Rising Pillar of Smoke / Ramy Ditzanny

My lines of protest were all taken as the act of a leftist masturbator
and I was only whispering. Irrelevancies. Spoiled words. What a waste of time.
And what have you done for the State, tiny-poet with droplet letters
concatenating poems for fat officers for stubborn oxen for thick-skinned
    desert lizards?

So that's what I did and now it's too late and this ugly madness can't
be stopped when the flag of blood-black and olive in the white-dust ruins
of the demolished house is wrapped in the prayer-shawl flag of deaf
and stubborn sacred sacrificial lambs, blue-white
they link arms and shoot in the village squares in a parade the band playing
a desperate march straight onto the landmine—the column of fireandcloud-gas-
chemicalwarfare-furnace ready for a sign a signal of activation

and I am a delicate man but I'll not flee, I'll sit here in the dark
and wait for first light in the sealed bathroom I'll shed a tear
I'll pray an innocent prayer before the squashed-heads
before the desert generation before the dumb herd:
Please forgive them, ancient and vengeful God, God of Armies, God of War!
Give them back a drop of *yiddishkeit* compassion contrition wistful humor
also a dash of chosen earth-salt for the Chosen People, the wise Jewish mind

From the edges of the East, sulfur spills
its poison mushroom seven times brighter than the light of the sun

Translated by Rachel Tzvia Back

Lullaby / Dahlia Ravikovitch

Mama and Grandma
will sing you a song,
your shining white mothers
will sing you a song,
Mama's shawl brushes
your bed with its wing.
Mama and Grandma
a mournful old tune
will sing in Jibalia's cordon of gloom.
There they sat, clinging together as one:
Papa wrecked, coughing up
blood from his lung,
his son of fifteen embracing his frame
like a steel hoop girding
his father's crushed form
—what little remained.
True loves,
sweet doves.
Thus did their captors make mock of them.

Mama and Grandma
will sing you a song
so you, sweet child,
may sleep without harm.
Rachel is weeping aloud for her sons.
A lamentation. A keening of pain.
When thou art grown and become a man,
the grief of Jibalia thou shalt not forget
the torment of Shati thou shalt not forget,
Hawara and Beita,
Jelazoun, Balata,
their cry still rises night after night.

Translated by Chana Bloch and Chana Kronfeld

That / Ronny Someck

That the mind is the body's commander-in-chief
That the body hides lust in the genital cave
That the genitals wet the prisoner's lips
That the prisoner is a broken tooth in the mouth that shouted the command
That the command knows neither limit nor border
That the border is stretched taut like a sock
That the sock is silent
That the silence unravels threads from the tangles of words
That in the mind words are stuck like a fence
And that behind them nothing is left to discuss

Translated by Vivian Eden

The Reason to Live Here / Aharon Shabtai

This country is turning into the private estate of twenty families.

Look at its fattened political arm, at the thick neck of its bloated bureaucracy:
these are the officers of Samaria.

There's no need to consult the oracle:
What the capitalist swine leaves behind, the nationalist hyena shreds with its
     teeth.

When the Governor of the Bank of Israel raises the interest rate by half-a-
     percent
the rich are provided with backyard pools by the poor.

The soldier at the outpost guards the usurer, who'll put a lien on his home
when he's laid off from the privatized factory and falls behind on his
     mortgage payments.

The pure words I suckled from my mother's breasts: Man, Child, Justice, Mercy,
     and so on,
are dispossessed before our eyes, imprisoned in ghettos, murdered at check-
     points.

And yet, there's still a good reason to stay on and live here—
to hide the surviving words in the kitchen, in the basement, or the bathroom.

The prophet Melampus saved twin orphaned snakes from the hand of his slaves:
they slithered toward his bed while he slept, then licked the auricles of his ears.
When he woke with a fright, he found he could follow the speech of birds—

so Hebrew delivered will lick the walls of our hearts.

Translated by Peter Cole

VIII

Things That Have No End

[Oh, let the darkness cover our eyes!] / Tuvia Ruebner

Oh, let the darkness cover our eyes!
Where can we flee from the sound of our hearts
proclaiming: It was our hands that spilt our blood!
To where can we still run from ourselves?

Translated by Rachel Tzvia Back

[The heart is parched] / Tuvia Ruebner

The heart is parched. The dirty blood shines.
You, me, he.
What we have done even God, full of compassion, will not forgive.
And the panicked run wild through a city of terror.

Translated by Rachel Tzvia Back

With the Steel Point of a Thorn / Zvi Atzmon

And thorns and thistles shall
grow there, all the land shall be
thorn and thistle, devouring
thorn-bush and brier, on the land of my people
briers will rise up.

The sin of Judah is written with an iron pen,
engraved with the steel point of a thorn.

Translated by Rachel Tzvia Back

Author's Note: This text is an interweaving, word for word, of descriptions of destruction from the books of Isaiah and Jeremiah (Isaiah 5:6; 7:24; 9:17; 32:13 and Jeremiah 17:1). The weaving work is dedicated to N.Z.

Now Is the Time / Liat Kaplan

And if trouble ensues
and we demand a life for a life
an eye for an eye
a tooth for a tooth
a hand for a hand
a foot for a foot
a burn for a burn
a wound for a wound
a bruise for a bruise
an eye for a tooth for a hand for a foot for a wound for a burn for a bruise
    for a life

for a life
and all the people witness the thunder

we'll make an altar of earth
trouble will ensue
and we'll stand far off
and there will be the cloud and the darkness
and we will not approach each other all night long.

Translated by Rachel Tzvia Back

Victim Again / Tuvia Ruebner

Being a victim, again and again—
what a task! Here and there both.
A victim begets a victimizer, victimizer begets a knife
a knife begets fear, fear
begets hatred, hatred—wickedness
and wickedness like locusts greedily eat

parcel after parcel of a land
bleeding like the feet of Jesus on the cross,
hobbling on crutches, trudging along
on wheelchairs, blind—

In Khan Younis five children on their way to school stepped on something.
In one second they became torn and ragged flesh. A sixth child was shot there
the same day, on the twenty third of November 2001. The army . . . is
checking . . . investigating . . . from that same spot . . . artillery fire was shot . . .
expresses . . . deep . . . sorrow . . .

The wagtail is again rising and falling, rising and falling on air currents,
the warbler is warbling in the bushes, and the robin too has been spotted.

Who else hears something in this terrible noise

Fear and hatred and hatred and fear
contempt of hatred and fear

But how do we end something that has no end?

Translated by Rachel Tzvia Back

One from Here / Salman Masalha

A poem for the late hours of the night

It changes so fast,
the world. And for me it's
now absurd. Things have got
to the point that I've stopped
thinking about fall. Because, after all, from here,
there's nowhere to go.
And anyway, even in the park
the trees are uprooted and gone.

And at times like these, it's dangerous
to go out in the streets in this country.
The road is so wet.
Blood flows in the main artery.
I count them:
One from here, one from there.
I count them
like sheep, until
I fall asleep.

Translated by Vivian Eden

Song of Praise / Tamir Greenberg

You, pure Wickedness, sublime Perpetuum Mobile of destruction agony and
    loss,
have you blessed Progress as it elevates your speech to art form?
Bless, Wickedness, the marvel of the plane, a lump of black steel
carried along swift currents of air, its greased belly laden
with brilliant metallic eggs, joyous Easter for the children of Belgrade.
Bless the gun barrel, sensitive and sharp-eyed,
granting eternal marble glory in a central square
even to a poor and simple youth of no remarkable talent.
Bless and extol science leaping onward. Bless Chemistry, Physics, Biology
as they propagate their wisdom in cheery yellow vapors
over cities, villages, and refugee camps.
Bless, Wickedness, the joy of deportation, the beauty of exile, the grace of
    genocide
and the burning of villages—more dear to despots than any palace or escort
    girl.
Rejoice in Kosovo and in Hebron, in Auschwitz and in Hiroshima,
excellent cities where you found refuge.
Bless as well the coming generation. Bless the son of the migrant laborer,
his warm and innocent flesh inviting lesions, sorrow, and disease.
Bless as well his father and mother, perched on the front line of quick profits
for the people of the Promised Land. Bless the love of God renewed in human
    hearts
at the turn of the millennium, for no gun or cannon can bequeath
the splendor of a sacred psalm.
Bless television that disseminates your divine work all around the globe.
Bless me, please, and those like me, persons of heart and morality,
comfortably seated in their rooms, composing a broken line,
bathing in the richness of metaphor.

Bless, Wickedness, bless, bless.
Bloom, Wickedness, bloom and prosper.
Rub your palms contentedly
as you contemplate human industry,
for great things are coming your way.

Translated by Tsipi Keller

Call in the Snakes / Tali Latowicki

And our camp was pure

Call in the snakes, as the pillagers have come—
they've come from our midst, and for what they've lost
they want to exact punishment.
They've come from cliffs and caves and dirt burrows
they've blocked up the wells and shot the donkey
they've torn up the travel passes
they've smashed the rifle butt into the child's cheek
they've stripped off Ibrahim's clothes and ransacked his food.
Call in the snakes, let them come and undo the strings of their hearts,
for their heart is defiled, and there's no cure.
Call in the snakes, let them come and pluck out my eyes,
for I am weary and have no desire to see.

Pray for the snakes, maybe their mouths hold the remedy—
call in the snakes and they'll protect us and remove the curse,
wreathlike they'll adorn our foreheads with forked tongues
whispering words of comfort at our temples, for we
are most beautiful in our death.

Translated by Rachel Tzvia Back

Order of the Day / Yitzhak Laor

Remember
that which
Amalek did,
to you of course,
Over.
Do unto Amalek
what Amalek
did, to you
of course, *Over.*

If you can't
find yourself
an Amalek, call
Amalek whomever
you want to do
to him what
Amalek did,
to you of course,
Over.

Don't compare
anything
to what Amalek
did, to you
of course, *Over.*
Not when
you want to do
that which
Amalek did,
to you of course,
Over and Out,
Remember.

Translated by Gabriel Levin

Good Intentions / Natan Zach

They had good intentions
when they tortured him. The machine was new,
fitting each body perfectly, like a glove,
the column of flame shone with a kind of luster
that could be called ethical
as it ploughed measured furrows in the flesh,
it was also expert in breaking bones,
it was unequaled in accuracy: bone after bone
like a chicken. The sounds of the cracking
echoed in the damp cellar,
and even the dampness did not come from bad intentions, God forbid—
this was what they had been given. After all,
it was necessary to be on guard against peeping toms and the press.
All in all, it must be said that given the budget, their work
wasn't bad, disposing of the bodies
wasn't their responsibility. For that another group
took over. Above all, we must praise
their devotion to the task. It was only because of this
that the slightest hint didn't leak
until it was too late and then not even God, in all His glory,
had he been there, would have been able to interfere
or to fix anything. Not that there was anything, God forbid,
to put right. They worked with a thoroughness that was Swiss
or Japanese, a total commitment to getting the job done.
What more can you ask of people?
These days, we know all this to be fairy tales
for young children, not the kind of thing that gave us
television, computers, or cannon fodder.
But then in those days you could still find people,
good souls they were called, a forgotten species,
who would gather in public places and unfurl their banners.

In general, the authorities tolerated them, only
rarely sending in mounted police or shooting
at them with rubber bullets or canisters of tear gas, it's only tears,
look, they caused no harm, said the wholly respectable *paterfamilias*. These
were the same who fathered the best soldiers, the most disciplined of all,
even those who took part in the great campaign of 2005,
came from conservative households, old-fashioned places, with pianos. To
show you that the truest adage is the one that says

that virtue comes from necessity, or necessity from virtue,
or however the saying goes.

Today all this is history, it barely makes it
into the books. What's the point of writing sentimental tales? Besides, there is
no demand for it, otherwise
it would have been published. After all, censorship was abolished
over forty years ago. The only censors who remain
are the ones assigned to the transvestites.
Those are still useful. Firstly, they serve as a warning
to the squeamish. Secondly, they can be put to use at festivals
and on national holidays, including costume parties. And thirdly, one
must take into account the pressure of the fashion industry.
Uniforms are not enough, no sir, this
we learned long ago in the same tortured way
that brought us to this point, a path survived only
by those with nerves of steel.

So let the new beauty rising out of the ashes flourish.
Without it, we couldn't even dream of the annual
improvements in the parades and the military reviews we
witness almost every year. These days we don't even conserve electricity
like those idiots did. And if we need another thousand trumpets,
we don't worry about logistics or the budget.
Really, all that belongs to our past of failure
when we still played all the old games
and hauled out those worn figures of speech
that are used today only for telling jokes.
After all is said and done, life is not a game, and you have to consider
the obstacles and dangers. He who goes to sleep contentedly on a full stomach
is apt to find himself missing a stomach in the morning, as the old joker
used to say. In the final analysis the short life is the good life,
there's no reason to prolong it artificially,
which also does not benefit the greater good. The most important thing
is that men recognize the objective, are ready for the necessary sacrifice, and
the next generation will accomplish what we, this generation,
didn't manage to complete.

Translated by Mark Braverman

Everything Must Go Back / Rami Saari

Everything must go back:
all the compositions to the students,
the spilt blood to the veins,
the territories will return to earth
and all the victims to wars,
and again, everything must go back:
to the students all the compositions,
to sperm all its shapes,
meaningful words to useless talk,
unwilling ears to explanations,
and since we are giving everything back,
we'll give seed back to conception,
and the fetus to the umbilicus,
kidnapped children to their mothers' wombs,
fallen crowns to their previous heads.
We shall certainly give back everything,
returning lost letters to orthography,
God all His lands,
the territories to earth
and the wilderness to the wilderness.
The world is a rolling wheel,
and time seems to be on its way
to return all that cannot be forbidden
to the righteous and the evil.
Everything must go back:
the crying voice to the desert,
the soul to its Creator,
and the universe, the entire entity,
to Immense Time
starting now.

Translated by Lisa Katz

You and We / Meir Wieseltier

You and we are the sauce of Western delicacies
so the baby herring in Amsterdam will be more tender
so the nostrils of the taster in the Bordeaux winery will dilate in rapture
so the sculptures which faded in Paris and London will be gilded again
so Scandinavian design will challenge Italian design
so fresh salmon steak will glow in splendor in Scotland
so top fashion houses can innovate each season
so major league teams will get an ultramodern stadium
so abandoned power stations will house fabulous museums
so Belgium will have countless brands of beer
so Venice won't sink and Berlin can return to its former glory
so dark-red Spanish dried ham and German sausage won't disappoint their fans
so hunters in England won't be deprived of their hobby—
you and we must become bloodthirsty beasts:
you must blow yourself up aboard buses crawling in our cities
turn wretched people and tender girls into steaks
and we must shoot smart missiles from helicopters through your alleys
to blast cars into dust and passers-by into coal-dolls
you must shoot rounds of fire at infants in highchairs in restaurants
divide our poor world into *dar-al-islam* and *dar-al-harb*
to rouse in your tender children eternal hatred and a drugged rapture for death
and we must stop women in labor from getting to doctors until the fetus dies
and shoot bent-over fathers sneaking across to find day work
we must uproot olives at harvest blow up houses of the poor
rave over our revelries in Hebron
polarize local humanity into Jew and Goy
two breeds of dogs—trained to kill.

Translated by Shirley Kaufman

(In Reply to the Question What Are You Still Doing Here) / Liat Kaplan

What are you doing here? There's nothing to see. Go on, get lost. Go, go already,

it's over. What is there for you here? Only growing darkness. They don't speak your language.

A different language, dissembling, says: Sky. Sea. What, what do you see?

The shining light is setting. The intoxicating scent of the mountain's soil is the scent of decay.

The streaming beauty of your city streets is infected. Go, go forth from your country

and from your homeland. Go to any other country, to a foreign tongue. It is

almost too late. Go forth. Here the vessels are cracked. Don't you see? Night descends. Tomorrow

the sun will not rise. Do you see what I see? Does it hurt? It hurts.

The sunset is adorned with a terrible orange. How awful is this place, our home.

It is nothing other than the house of God, it is a graveyard. Redder than can be borne.

Ravenous ravenous. What are you still doing here? Love ruins

the line. Word for word write on your vessels: Here, all

is nothing. You see. What are you saying? Go forth. Go.

Do you see what I see? Love is blind. Get out of here,

even the sea is retreating. Why brood on the edges of the wound?

Translated by Rachel Tzvia Back

Then We Didn't Yet Know / Dahlia Falah

Then we didn't yet know
that the Occupation would be forever.
Even when it would be forcibly extracted like a tooth
and tossed behind electric fences
and magnetic crossings
while cement and petrol magnates
traveled from Ramallah to Gaza—
even then it would be remembered longingly—
how young it was, the Occupation,
composed only of Arab women bent over tomatoes
in Jewish fields, men with nylon bags
waiting for work at the Ashkelon junction,
jumping into grey service Peugots,
and the Secret Service men who lived three to a villa in Afridar
actually changing their license plates to army license plates before
going off to work, so they wouldn't be identified.
It was young. In the restaurants they peeled vegetables into large tins, then
fried them, built on scaffolds. There were many organizations.
And they too were young:
volunteers with Chinese weapons, poets,
but the Occupation didn't recognize them,
because it was busy arguing in the classrooms whether to return territories or not,
and Ofer P., whose father was wounded in the Battle of Jenin,
and had shrapnel stuck in his back,
said: "In any case, there'll be another war."
That's what his father taught him.
That's how young the Occupation was,
and look at it now.

Translated by Rachel Tzvia Back

IX

What May Yet Heal

from Houses (Plural); Love (Singular) / Yehuda Amichai

How they'll exploit our love! How they'll trace the line of your thighs
and the line of my arm on their maps to mark the borders between lands
we didn't know existed, how the color of your eyes and the color of my eyes
will flutter in the flags of new nations in the world of the future.
And with the words we said to one another in the night they'll craft
secret contracts and declarations of independence and treaties of surrender
     and victory.
How they'll exploit us! From our lovemaking positions
they'll invent the clever new machines of the next century
and from our motions of love, someone perhaps will organize a large
military operation, an embrace, a clasping, a grasping, pincers, missile
     trajectories.
And from our love's repose they'll make final reckonings
and visions of the end of days, fine and calm,
in our enduring silence and everlasting love.

Translated by Mark Braverman

from In a Collapsing House / Maxim Gilan

♦ Child

Nationality? None.
Your homeland belongs to whom?

Here where you refuse
to settle accounts with eternity.
The soldiers carry out their orders
arrogantly
commanding shackles
for Zion
spreading the plague.
Their vague
steps slack as they approach the bulldozer—
on a freezing day, nothing will sway
them:

Not the baby's screams nor the woman's raw cries—
law
of the legions is law.
The crocodile-teeth crunch
the front-door planks into dust
and the dreams of girls
who only yesterday were seen
looking out
from the now
frameless window.

♦ Bulldozer

It bites even
into the floor. Into the flora. Into the plate
of spoiled hummus. Into the plastic bucket, into the cupboard
of ragged clothes
into the songs the Hebrews sang
when the country first sprang
up. Into the despair
and disgrace. Into the soldiers' certainty of place
and purity of arms and doing no wrong,

into satisfaction and fireside songs
and also into rusted tin pots and pans.

Damn—
dammit, Mama—
they are beating children with clubs, with Gods
(and my son, if you weren't one of them, they
would be beating you too).

◆ The House Is Resurrected
The house collapsed—
the charge was detonated by the window
facing the view.
Now, dusty ruins hide the landscape
that a brief moment before breathed, dreamed.
Now the tree outside
is covered and sealed: loftier
than all other nations
it is sung to
by the bulldozer scooping up
the collapsing house. You see,
only a miracle
can still save us here
from drunken victory.

But if
we were suddenly saved
from our awful victory,
then we would all wake up in the land of dreams.
The house would rise high
on its foundations,
return
from its ruins.
And the righteous of the earth
would enter the house and set a table,
planting around it a garden

of rare and fragrant flowers. Date trees
and olives would again grow all around, so masculine
and eastern

and again the scent of hot winds would fill our lungs
with the perfume of orchards—
a small woman, blowing on the nape of our necks.

♦ The Landscape Also Awakens

Roads
and highways will disappear from the landscape.
The house, there, close to the beach
will rise up and shake itself like a hairy beast
entangled in spiderwebs. And quickly
like lights suddenly switched off,
road after road will disappear
as butterflies of night and day
again fill the skies
of the land of the shadow-of-death
and Ruth
and Abed
lie down together with love and courage
in a field of clover.

Translated by Rachel Tzvia Back

Under the Olive Tree / Asher Reich

The light of the olive in this tree
is thick and dark—
lost blood flows in it.

When I sat under its leaves
time killed itself in the tree's shade.
All the long afternoon
a figure on the hill

watched me, her face covered with a veil—
and the sun, like me, searched for her eyes
all the long afternoon,
the flute of silence singing in the rocks
as I gnawed nervously on the heavy air.

Years passed between us in fire—
an abundance of blood did not extinguish it.
With straight-necked weariness
we raised dust in our bodies—
but what connects us here
may yet be stitched back together
and heal.

Translated by Rachel Tzvia Back

Notes

Section I: And the Land, Will You Possess It All?

Rami Ditzanny / Cry the Beloved Country
Line 9: "I've become loathsome to myself," Cf. Numbers 11:20.
Line 11: Cf. Job 30:5.
Lines 12 & 14: Cf. Ezekiel 33:26 and Psalms 44:4.
Final line: Cf. Jeremiah 50:31: "Behold I am against thee, O thou most proud, saith the Lord God, for thy day is come." Also Cf. Amos 4:2: "Behold days are coming upon you." The verses that follow prophesize the exile of the Israelites, because of the abominations they have committed. Cf. also Jeremiah 19:6 and Isaiah 39:6.

Arik A. / Palestina—Eretz Yisrael
The reference in the title and body of the poem is to a debate that unfolded during the British Mandate of Palestine as to what the official name of the region would be. The mandate government wanted the name of the land they were ruling to be *Palestina*, while the Jewish residents (the Yishuv) wanted the name to be *Eretz Yisrael* ("the Land of Israel"—abbreviated as א"י Aleph-Yod). The compromise eventually achieved was that the initials 'Aleph-Yod' (א"י) for 'Eretz Yisrael' would be written in brackets whenever 'Palestina' was written.

Dotan Arad / [Palestinian souls]
Section 3, Line 14: Cf. Micha 4:3–4: "Nation shall not take up sword against nation, neither shall they learn war anymore. But they shall sit every man under his vine and under his fig tree; and none shall make them afraid."
Section 3, Final Line: The line is a direct quotation from the Mishna, Seder Nezikin, Tractate Avot, chapter 1:11.

Ramy Ditzanny / We'll Build Our Homeland, for This Land Is Ours
The title of the poem is taken from the opening lines of a prestate Israeli folk song, sung in the 1940s/1950s.

Line 9: *Falahim* is Arabic for peasant farmers.

Line 14: Cf. Exodus 1:11–12: "And [the Egyptians] set taskmasters over them to oppress them with forced labor, and [the Israelites] built garrison cities for Pharaoh...But the more they were oppressed, the more they increased and spread out."

Rami Saari / The Only Democracy (in the Middle East)
Line 6: Cf. 2 Samuel 2:14.
Line 8: Cf. Jeremiah 31:20.

Liat Kaplan / The Horizon's Clenched Mouth
Line 1: This line quotes from a famous haiku by seventeenth-century poet Matsuo Basho. The haiku in full is "A cicada shell; / it sang itself / utterly away." Translation into English is by R. H. Blyth.
Line 12: Cf. Numbers 13:32.

Dahlia Ravikovitch / Free Associating
Line 19: Cf. Leviticus 22:28: "And whether it be cow or ewe, ye shall not kill it and its young both in one day."
Line 24: "Our storehouses are filled with grain" is from a patriotic Israeli song from the 1950s, based on the verse from Proverbs 3:10: "So shall thy barns be filled with plenty, and thy presses shall burst out with new wine."
Line 25: A wadi is a riverbed that is dry except in the rainy season.
Lines 31–32: Zikhron Ya'akov and Mazkeret Batya were agricultural settlements in prestate Israel, established in 1882 under the patronage of Baron Edmund de Rothschild, a philanthropist also instrumental in the founding of Israel's wine industry.

Section II: The Arrogance of Our Self-Destruction

Moshe Dor / Asteroid
Line 7: Beit Ja'ala is a Palestinian town located five kilometers south of Jerusalem, on the road to Bethlehem and Hebron. The town has about fifteen thousand inhabitants, predominantly Christian, with a Muslim minority.
Line 8: Gilo is a Jewish residential neighborhood of about forty thousand people that lies within the municipal boundaries of Jerusalem. Gilo was built on lands occupied in the 1967 war.

Meir Wieseltier / Sonnet: Against Making Blood Speak Out
The Amorites and Amalekites were two Old Testament tribes with whom the Israelites had ongoing conflict and warfare. The Amalekites in particular have come to represent the archetypal enemy of the Jews.

Asher Reich / *from* some Israeli Thoughts
Section 2, Line 9: Cf. Joshua 5:6: "A land flowing with milk and honey."
Section 2, Line 10: A *tallit* is a Jewish prayer shawl.

Tuvia Ruebner / [Lice have conquered you]
Line 1: The phrase rendered here as "glorious Holy Land" is literally "Land of the Deer" in the Hebrew—a biblical appellation referring to the beauty and glory of the Holy Land of Israel. Cf. Daniel 11:16.

Dvora Amir / Woodcut of a Landscape
Line 1: The opening words are taken from a well-known Jewish song of longing for Jerusalem. The original Hebrew reads: "From above the peak of Mount Scopus, peace to you Jerusalem." Esaweya is a Palestinian village at the foothills of Mount Scopus, just beneath the Mount Scopus Hadassah Hospital (and maternity ward).
Line 4: Anatot is a Palestinian village east of Mount Scopus. It is also the place where Jeremiah prophesized. Cf. Jeremiah 1:1.

Oreet Meital / At the Edges of the East
Title: The title of the poem alludes to the third line of the Israeli national anthem "Hatikva" ("The Hope"), written by Naftali Herz Imber, a Galician Jew, and set to music in Palestine in the early 1880s. The anthem speaks about the exiled Jewish people looking eastward toward Zion, longing for a return to their homeland. The title of the poem changes the preposition of the third line of the anthem from "*toward* the edges of the East" to "*at* the edges of the East," signaling the post-exilic condition of the Jews.
Lines 2 & 8: *arei miskinot,* here rendered both as "wretched cities" (line 2) and "garrisoned cities" (line 8), is a biblical reference to the cities of storehouses and granaries the enslaved Israelites were forced to build for Pharaoh. Cf. Exodus 1:12. The Hebrew word *miskinot* (storehouses) is very similar in sound to the Hebrew word for wretchedness—*miskenut.*

Meir Wieseltier / The Tel-Aviv Subway
Title: There is no subway in Tel-Aviv. Bureaucracy, budget, and other priorities have prevented it from being built for more than forty years.

David Avidan / A Prayer to Allah Hashem God
Title: *Allah* is the Arabic name for God. *Hashem* is a Jewish name for God, the word meaning "The Name."

Section III: The Fruit Dies Before the Tree

Aryeh Sivan / Mite
Lines 20–21: These lines allude to the second line of the famous poem "My Heart is in the East," by twelfth-century Andalusian Hebrew poet Yehuda Halevi. Halevi's line reads: "How can I possibly taste what I eat? How could it please me?" This poem, and many others by Halevi, speaks of his longing for Zion.
Line 22: The "West" alludes to the Diaspora and evokes the first line of Halevi's poem: "My heart is in the East—and I am at the edge of the West." The translations of the lines by Halevi are by Peter Cole in his anthology *The Dream of the Poem: Hebrew Poetry From Muslim and Christian Spain 950–1492* (Princeton: Princeton University Press, 2007), p. 164.

Tal Nitzan / Torn
Line 24: "arise, get thee out" (*kumi tsiee*) is taken from the third stanza of the Friday night prayer Lecha Dodi. In this verse, the Sabbath queen is enjoined to rise up out of destruction and to leave the Valley of Tears.

Aharon Shabtai / To Dr. Majed Nassar
Dr. Nassar is a prominent physician and public health official from the Palestinian town of Beit Sahour, near Bethlehem.

Dahlia Ravikovitch / The Story of the Arab Who Died in the Fire
In an 1996 interview with the news daily *Yediot Acharonot*, Ravikovitch said: "As to the [poem about the Palestinian] dayworker [from the Occupied Territories], when Jews nailed shut the door of the warehouse where he was sleeping, so he couldn't get out when it was set on fire—I wrote that poem because I understand the fear he felt before he was saved by death."

Yitzhak Laor / Kaddish
Title: The Kaddish is the Jewish prayer for the dead, spoken at the funeral, during the year-long period of mourning and on the anniversary of the death.

Section IV. The Hands—They Were the Hands of Soldiers

Aharon Shabtai / Toy Soldiers
Line 3: Rafi'ah is a neighborhood in Gaza.

Admiel Kosman / Poem for Muhammad
The title refers to twelve-year-old Palestinian Muhammad al-Durrah who was killed in October 2000 in a shootout between IDF troops and Palestinian mili-

tants. The images of Muhammad—still alive, crouching behind his father and desperately seeking safety—were shown around the world.

Yitzhak Laor / Calf
Title: The reference is to the calf who is being led to slaughter in the plaintive Yiddish folk song "Dona Dona." The refrain of the song is "Dona Dona." The music to this song was written by Sholem Secunda (1894-1974) and the lyrics by Aaron Zeitlin (1889–1974). The song was translated into Hebrew and English both and is sung as a folk song.

Amir Or / There Is a God
Line 3: Shuafat, a well-off Palestinian village northeast of Jerusalem, straddles the Jerusalem municipal border.

Section V: And If the Dead Is a Child, Will Someone Gather Him Up?

Aharon Shabtai / To a Pilot
Line 3: Jenin is a Palestinian city in the northern West Bank and home to a large refugee camp founded there in 1953. Large parts of Jenin were destroyed in an IDF attack in May 2002.

Aryeh Sivan / I Protest
Title & Line 1: The Hebrew words for "I protest" (*ani mocheh*) mean also "I wipe away."
Line 11: The reference here is to the biblical Joseph and his coat of many colors—in the Hebrew original referred to as "a robe of stripes" (*kutonet pasim*). Cf. Genesis 37:3.
Lines 15 & 19: Cf. Genesis 37:5–7, 13. The biblical city of Shechem was located where the modern-day Palestinian city of Nablus now sits. Nablus is still called Shechem in Hebrew.
Lines 19–21: Cf. Genesis 37:31–33.

Yosef Ozer / Coke and Jeans
Line 3: Cf. Genesis 16:5–6.
Line 10: Cf. Genesis 16:7.
Line 13: Cf. Genesis 22.

Maya Bejerano / [Stripes of light on the wall]
On March 4, 1996, on the eve of the Purim festival, a suicide bomber blew himself up outside the Dizengoff shopping center in Tel-Aviv. Thirteen Israelis

were killed, more than 130 wounded, with many children among the dead and wounded both. Purim is a Jewish holiday geared especially toward children and involves the wearing of costumes.

Oreet Meital / October 2000
Title: October 2000 of the poem's title refers to the starting date of the Al-Aksa Intifada. On September 30, 2000, twelve-year-old Palestinian Muhammad al-Durrah was shot and killed at the Al Shuhada Junction, while trying to return home with his father. As mentioned earlier, the images of Muhammad—still alive, crouching behind his father and desperately seeking safety—were aired around the world.
Section 1, Line 12: Jewish legend has it that the flesh of the Leviathan, a fantastic sea monster, is reserved as food for the rightous in the next world.
Section 2, Line 12: Cf. Joshua 2:11.

Yitzhak Laor / The Love of Truth
Twelve-year-old Muhammad al-Durra was shot at the Al Shuhada Junction, while trying to return home with his father. Video footage of Muhammad trying to hide in his father's arms from IDF fire was aired the world round. Muhammad died at the junction, in his father's arms, as ambulances were not allowed into the area to evacuate him for medical care.

Dan Daor / The Man Who Apparently Caused the Death of Hilmi Shusha
Title: Hilmi Susha was an eleven-year-old Palestinian boy who was clubbed to death with a rifle by Nachum Korman, an Israeli settler, in 1997. Korman served eight months in jail on a charge of manslaughter.
Line 5: Baruch Goldstein was an American-Israeli physician who on February 25, 1994, Purim day, killed 29 Muslims and injured 125 in a shooting attack in the Cave of the Patriarchs/Ibrahimi Mosque in Hebron, West Bank. The Palestinians were kneeling in prayer when Goldstein slaughtered them, A book in praise of Goldstein and written by his followers was titled *Baruch Ha'Gever* ("Blessed Is the Man [or Manly])." Over the years, Baruch Goldstein's grave has become a pilgrimage site for Jewish right-wing extremists.
Line 11: The reference is to the Knesset member, of the National Religious Party, Hanan Porat, who entered the emergency meeting of the Judea and Samaria Council on the morning of the 1994 Goldstein Massacre with greetings of "Happy Purim."
Lines 15–16: The reference is to Achav, king of Samaria, who caused the death of Navot the Jezreelite Navot and then took possession of his vineyard. Cf. I Kings 21, particularly verse 19: "Thus said the Lord: Would you murder and take possession too? Thus said the Lord: In the very place where the dogs lapped up Navot's blood, the dogs will lap up your blood too."

Sharron Hass / The Day of Blood

In 1997, Hilmi Shusha—an eleven-year-old Palestinian boy—was clubbed to death with a rifle by Nachum Korman, an Israeli settler. Korman served eight months in jail on a charge of manslaughter.

Yitzhak Laor / Landscape with Fear in the Eye

Line 12: For "be fruitful and multiply," cf. Genesis 1:28.

Lines 19-20: A *dunam* is a measure of land, equal to approximately a quarter acre.

Line 28: "Soldiers in Arab disguise" is *mista'aravim* in Hebrew. The reference is to an elite IDF commando unit composed of Israeli soldiers who disguise themselves as Arabs in order to infiltrate Palestinian towns and villages. The word *mista'arev*, literally "to become Arabized," predates the intifada but took on a new meaning once adopted by the military.

Final Line: "The valley is a dream" is the title and first line of a prestate Israeli folk song written by S. Shalom (also known as Shalom Yosef Shapira) and put to music by Moshe Rappaport. The song speaks about sleeping among the grapevines in the valley and from there watching the sunrise.

Section VI: He Who Demolishes a Person's Home

Yoram Levi Porat / Fifteen Minutes to *Khurban Ha'Bayit*

Line 13: Cf. Psalms 42:2: "As the hart panteth after the water brooks, so panteth my soul after thee, O God."

Line 31: The Egyptian born Umm Kulthum (1904–1975) was and is one of the best known and most beloved singers in the Arab world.

Diti Ronen / Curfew, Variation #5

Line 12: *Mansaf* is a Bedouin dish consisting of Arabic rice, a rich broth made from dry sour milk (*jameed*), and either lamb or chicken.

Avner Treinin / *from* The Olive

Final line: for Kerem-Navot, cf. Kings 1:21.

Rachel Dana / There Is No One Here

Line 2: Armon Ha'Natziv, also known as East Talpoit, is an eastern neighborhood of Jerusalem. The lands of Armon Ha'Natziv were captured and annexed to Jerusalem in the 1967 war. The term means "The governor's mansion" and refers to the complex of buildings in which the British high commissioner of Palestine resided during the Mandate period.

Line 12: A-Tur is a Palestinian village situated on the Mount of Olives, in East Jerusalem. The village of A-Tur was annexed to Israel, along with all of East Jerusalem, in 1967, by the Jerusalem municipality, a move reaffirmed in 1980 by the Israeli Parliament.

Avner Treinin / From the Songs of *Tu B'Shevat*—The Festival of Tree Planting

Title: Tu B'Shevat, the fifteenth day of the Jewish month of Shevat (which usually falls in February), is the Jewish "New Year for Trees." It is one of the four Jewish new years. The holiday, traditionally marked by the planting of trees in Israel, is a favorite among the children and has many children's songs associated with it.

Section VII: Sing for Us from the Songs of Zion

Dahlia Ravikovitch / Our Captors Required of Us a Song

The title of the poem and its first line—like the epigraph taken from Lea Goldberg's "From the Songs of Zion"—are taken from Psalm 137, which opens with the famous phrase "By the rivers of Babylon . . ." The lines "we have hung your lyres / far away / on the willows" are a revision of verse 2 from this same psalm.

Ramy Ditzanny / The Rising Pillar of Smoke

Title: "Rising," *mitabech* in the Hebrew, is written as an acronym, which alludes to the army term for gas-biological-chemical warfare (*abach*).
For "pillar of smoke," cf. Judges 20:38–40. The Hebrew word for smoke, *ashan*, rhymes with the word for cloud, *anan*, and through the sound associations, the title alludes also to the pillar of cloud which God put before the Israelites as they left Egypt, to guide them in their exodus. Cf. Exodus 13:21: "The Lord went before them in a pillar of cloud by day, to guide them along the way, and in a pillar of fire by night, to give them light, that they might travel day and night."
Line 20: "From the edges of the east" is taken from the Israeli anthem "Hatikva" ("The Hope").

Dahlia Ravikovitch / Lullaby

Line 9: Jibalia is the largest Palestinian refugee camp in the Gaza Strip, just north of Gaza City, a focal point of resistance to the occupation.
Line 19: "captors," cf. Psalm 137:3, "For there they that carried us away captive required of us a song."
Lines 24–25: "Rachel . . . lamentation," cf. Jeremiah 31:15, "lamentation and bitter weeping; Rachel, weeping for her children, refused to be comforted."
Lines 27–28: "Thou shalt not forget," cf. Deuteronomy 25:19, upending the command to "blot out the remembrance of Amalek," Israel's archenemy.

Line 28: Shati is a refugee camp in the Gaza Strip.

Line 29: Hawara is a village south of Nablus in the West Bank. Beita is a village in the West Bank, near the Israeli border.

Line 30: Jelazoun is a refugee camp near Ramallah in the West Bank. Balata is a refugee camp on the outskirts of Nablus in the West Bank.

Line 31: "their cry," cf. 1 Samuel 5:12, "the cry of the city went up to heaven."

Aharon Shabtai / The Reason to Live Here

Line 3: Samaria was the capital of the northern kingdom of Israel in the ninth and eight centuries B.C.E., following the split of the Israelite kingdom after the death of Solomon. This is now the Hebrew name for the northern part of the West Bank, in the biblicizing terminology of the Greater Israel movement and the Israeli government.

Line 14: In Greek mythology, Melampus was the first mortal endowed with prophetic powers (Bullfinch). The story of the serpents in told in *Apollodorus* I:9.11.

Section VIII: Things That Have No End

Tuvia Ruebner / [Oh, let the darkness cover our eyes!]

Line 3: Cf. Deuteronomy 21:7: "It was not our hands that shed this blood." Ruebner changes the *lo* ("no" or "not") of the biblical verse into *halo*, "indeed [it is]" or "is it not."

Tuvia Ruebner / [The heart is parched]

Line 3: "God, full of compassion" (*El maleh rahamim*) is the opening of the Hebrew prayer for the dead spoken at graveside.

Zvi Atzmon / With the Steel Point of a Thorn

Title & final line: *B'tsiporen shamir* is taken from Jeremiah 17:1. The word *shamir* works in three ways in the Hebrew. It means "thorn," as is repeated throughout the poem, and also "flint" or emery. Finally, the poet is alluding also to Yitzhak Shamir, the prime minister of Israel during the early days of the first intefadah. Within this context, *b'tsiporen shamir* means also "in the claws of Shamir."

Liat Kaplan / Now Is the Time

Lines 1-9: Cf. Exodus 21: 23–25.

Line 12: Cf. Exodus 20:14. The description is of the Israelites upon their receiving the Ten Commandments.

Line 14: Cf. Exodus 20:19.

Line 16: Cf. Exodus 20:14, 17.

Tuvia Ruebner / Victim Again

Line 11: Khan Younis is a city and refugee camp in the southern part of the Gaza Strip. The refugee camp was founded in 1948 and initially held 35,000 refugees, mostly from deracinated Palestinian villages in the Beer Sheva area. The number of refugees (including descendants) registered with UNRWA in mid-2002 was 60,662. Khan Younis has been the target of frequent raids by the IDF, and heavy battles have ensued in the area.

Tali Latowicki / Call in the Snakes

The title of the poem is taken from a poem of the same name by Haim Nachman Bialik (1873–1934), often considered the greatest Hebrew poet of modern times. The entire poem is in dialogue with Bialik's angry and apocalyptic text.

Yitzhak Laor / Order of the Day

The Amalekites were an Old Testament tribe with whom the Israelites had ongoing conflict and warfare. The Amalekites have come to represent the archetypal enemy of the Jews.

Lines 1–4: Cf. Deuteronomy 25:17, "Remember what Amalek did to you on your journey, after you left Egypt," and 25:19, "You shall blot out the memory of Amalek from under heaven. Do not forget."

Meir Wieseltier / You and We

Line 20: *Dar-al-islam* and *dar-al-harb* (Arabic) are Islamic terms used by extremist ideologists. Their literal meaning is: "the house of Islam" and "the house of war." The idea is that the world is divided in two: territories that are Islamic already and territories that true believers should strive to conquer or Islamize by Holy War, Jihad.

Liat Kaplan / (In Reply to the Question What Are You Still Doing Here)

The "you" of the poem is in the female form (*at*), as is the voice of the first-person speaker.

Line 5: Cf. Genesis 12:1, where God instructs Abraham to leave his home.

Lines 9–10: "How awful is this place" and "It is nothing other than the house of God" are direct quotations from Genesis 28:17.

Final line: The word for "edge," *safah*—means also "shore," "lips," and "language."

Dahlia Falah / Then We Didn't Yet Know

Lines 12 & 14: Ashkelon is an Israeli town just north of the Gaza Strip. Afridar is a neighborhood of villas in Ashkelon. The Gaza Strip was occupied by Israel from 1967 until the unilateral disengagement of August 2005.

Biographical Notes

Poets

Arik A. is the author of *Confession* (1994), *Map of the Beloved Homeland* (2001), and *A Post-War Evening* (2003). His most recent poetry volume, *Vagabond*, was published in early 2006. His seminal article on the early work of the Hebrew poet Uri Zvi Greenberg, "The Naked, the Hairy and the Primitive," was published in the critical anthology *A Poetic Option* (Carmel Press, 2006). Arik A. is one of the editors of the literary journal *Emdah* (*Position*).

Yehuda Amichai (1924–2000), was born in Wurzburg, Germany, to a religiously observant family, immigrated with his family to Israel in 1936, and settled in Jerusalem. In World War II he served with the British army's Jewish Brigade and later fought in the Palmach during Israel's 1948 War of Independence. Following the war, Amichai attended Hebrew University, where he studied biblical texts and Hebrew literature. His first volume of poetry, *Now and in Other Days*, published in 1955, immediately signaled a tidal wave of change in Hebrew poetry; this and subsequent volumes of poetry established Amichai as a leading voice in Hebrew poetry. In 1982 he received the Israel Prize, recognized for having "effected a revolutionary change in both the subject matter and the language of Hebrew poetry." In addition to thirteen books of poetry, Amichai published a collection of short stories, two novels, children's literature, and plays. Amichai was poet in residence at many universities, including Berkeley, New York University, and Yale, and received numerous awards in Israel and throughout the world, including Nobel Prize nominations. His work has been translated and published in forty languages and is included in high school and university syllabuses worldwide. His archives are kept at the Beinecke Rare Book and Manuscript Library of Yale University.

Dvora Amir, born in Jerusalem in 1948, is a graduate of the Hebrew University in Jerusalem, where she studied literature, Jewish philosophy and Kabbalah. She also studied American literature at the University of Illinois. Amir is the author of *Slow Burning* (1994) and *Documentary Poems* (2003), and her poems have appeared in numerous journals and magazines. Amir was a 2006 recipient of the Prime Minister's Award for Hebrew Writers and the 1995 Kugel Prize for Fine Literature.

Dotan Arad has published poems in various magazines including the religious literary journal *Meishiv Haruach*. Married with two children, Arad is currently writing his doctoral dissertation on the lives of Jews in Arab countries during the Mamaluk and the beginning of the Ottoman periods.

Zvi Atzmon, born in 1948, teaches Life Sciences at the David Yellin College in Jerusalem. He has published eight books of poetry and has received various awards, including the ACUM Prize (Israeli Composers, Authors and Publishers Association—1980, 1983, 1986, 2006), the Kugel Prize (1991), and the Prime Minister's Award (1992, 2000).

David Avidan (1934–1995) was one of Israel's leading poets and a major originator of contemporary avant-garde Israeli poetry. He published eighteen volumes of poetry, in addition to two plays and two books for children. Avidan received the Abraham Woursell Prize from the University of Vienna.

Maya Bejerano was born in 1949 in Kibbutz Eilon, near the northern border of Israel. She has produced twelve volumes of poetry, as well as two collections of stories, a play, a storybook for children, and a record of her poems set to music. She won the Prime Minister's Award twice (1986, 1994), the Israeli Prize for Poetry for both *The Hymns of Job* (1993) and *Trying to Touch My Belly-Button* (1997), and the Bialik Prize (2003). She lives in Tel-Aviv with her daughter.

Rahel Dana, born in Persia in 1956, studied theater, philosophy, and journalism at Tel-Aviv University. Her poetry has been published in numerous journals, including *Helicon, Carmel, Iton77*, and in the literary supplements of Israel's leading newspapers: *Haaretz, Davar,* and *Ma'ariv.* Her first poetry collection, *The Painful Beauty of the Morning*, was published in 2007 by Carmel Press.

Dan Daor, sinologist, translator, and critic, is senior editor at Xargol Books, the publishers of the Hebrew edition of *With an Iron Pen*.

Ramy Ditzanny earned degrees from Technion University and from the London Film School and is also a trained desert expedition guide. He is the author of five books of poetry and two books for children. He has received several awards, including the Tel-Aviv Award and the ACUM Prize.

Moshe Dor, born in Tel-Aviv in 1932, is the author of sixteen volumes of poetry and has also written six children's books, two collections of interviews with writers, and one volume of essays. Dor was Counselor for Cultural Affairs at the Israeli Embassy in London and Distinguished Writer-in-Residence at the American University in Washington, D.C. He has also coedited three English anthologies of contemporary Israeli poetry. Dor is a two-time recipient of the Prime Minister's Award for Literature, was awarded the Bialik Prize, and served as president of Israeli PEN. Three volumes of his work have been published in English translation: *Maps of Time* (1978), *Crossing the River* (1989), and *Khamsin: Memoirs and Poetry of a Native Israeli* (1994).

Shai Dotan was born in Eilat in 1969 and lives in Jerusalem. His translations and poems have appeared in numerous journals, including *Helicon* and *Carmel*, and in the *Haaretz* newspaper culture supplement. His first book, *On the Verge*, won the Education Minister's Prize for First Books (2005). Dotan is an economist in the public sector and moderates poetry workshops for youth and adults.

Gil Engelstein was born in Jerusalem in 1986, recently completed his army service in the IDF radio station, and has participated and published in the MATAN project, an Israeli program for young writers.

Dahlia Falah is a pen name, and details of her personal life are a secret closely guarded by her publisher. Her first poems appeared in the late 1970s, her first book in 1997, and her most recent publication, entitled *2003*, was published in 2003.

Maxim Gilan (1931–2005), poet, author, essayist, and critic, was born in France and was brought to Israel in 1944 with his mother and sister. He published eight collections of poetry and one collection of stories. Gilan's outspoken and constant criticism of the Israeli occupation, together with his struggle against Israeli censorship throughout the 1950s and 1960s, resulted in various periods of imprisonment and in his poetry books being shunned by the poetry establishment of the day. In 1969, Gilan left Israel to live in self-imposed exile in France, returning to Israel only in 1993. In 2004, Gilan received the Prime Minister's Prize and the Levi Eshkol Prize for Hebrew literature.

Tamir Greenberg was born in Tel Aviv in 1959. An architect, lecturer, playwright and poet, he also dabbles in physics. His work as poet and playwright has received many awards, including the Prime Minister's Award. He has published two poetry volumes: *Self Portrait with Quantum and a Dead Cat* (1993) and *The Thirsty Soul* (2002). His poems have been translated and published in many languages, among them Arabic, English, French, Spanish, German, and Russian. In 2007 his play *Hebron* was staged by Habima, Israel's national theater.

Sharron Hass is a poet and essayist. She has published three books: *The Mountain Mother Is Gone* (1997), *The Stranger and Everyday-Woman* (2001), and *Subjects* *of the Sun* (2006). Hass has received several awards, among them the Prime Minister's Award for Poetry (2003) and a Fulbright Scholarship for participation in the International Writers Program at the University of Iowa (2005). English translations of her poems have appeared in numerous literary magazines including *Trafika, Poetry International, Apokalipsa,* and *Chicago Review,* as well as in anthologies of contemporary Israeli poetry published in the United States.

Liat Kaplan, poet, editor, and leader of writing workshops, was born on a kibbutz and now lives in Tel Aviv. She studied at the Hebrew University in Jerusalem, the New School in New York, and Ben-Gurion University in Beer Sheva. She has published five volumes of poetry, in addition to twelve books and pamphlets on political and social issues. Since 2006, Kaplan has served as the artistic director of the annual Israeli Poets Festival in Metulla. Her most recent book, *In Praise of Forgetting,* was published by Carmel Press. For the last thirty years, Kaplan has taught and edited poetry books. She is the recipient of many awards, including the 2007 Prime Minister's Award.

Admiel Kosman, formerly professor of Talmud at Bar Ilan University in Israel, is now professor of Jewish Studies at Potsdam University and the Academic Director of Abraham Geiger College in Berlin. Born in Israel in 1957, Kosman is the author of eight books of poems, coeditor of the anthology of spiritual poetry *A New Song,* and writes a column on midrash for an Israeli newspaper.

Yitzhak Laor, born in 1948, is a poet, playwright, and novelist. He is the author of eight collections of poetry, three novels, two collections of short stories, three collections of essays, and one play. Laor is the founder and editor of *Mita'am,* a review of literature and radical thought. He holds a PhD in Theater and Literature from Tel-Aviv University.

Tali Latowicki, born 1976, received her master's degree from the Hebrew Literature department of Ben-Gurion University, Beer-Sheva. Currently, Latowicki is the editor of the *Masa Kritit,* a series of books researching Jewish and Israeli literature and culture published by Heksherim Institute and Kinneret-Zmora-Dvir Press. Her poems have been published in various anthologies and poetry journals and on the internet site *Shireshet.* Since 2003 Latowicki has been publishing poetry, articles, and reviews on her personal internet site, www.notes.co.il/talila.

Salman Masalha, bilingual author and poet, writes in Hebrew and Arabic. He was born in 1953 in the Galilee village of al-Maghar and moved to Jerusalem in 1972. He studied at the Hebrew University, focusing on classical Arabic poetry. His articles, poems, and translations have appeared in newspapers, magazines, and anthologies in Arabic and Hebrew and have also been translated into other languages. He has published seven poetry books, some of which have been translated into other languages. His latest book, *Mother Tongue* (in Arabic), was published in 2006. His book *In Place* was awarded the 2006 President's Prize for Hebrew Literature.

Gilad Meiri was born in Jerusalem in 1965 and has recently completed his doctorate on the work of Israeli poet David Avidan at Tel-Aviv University. His two poetry books are *Organic Paganic* (Carmel, 2003) and *Tremors in Jelly* (Carmel, 2006). Meiri received the Jerusalem Prize for his first collection and was a recipient of the Prime Minister's Award in 2008.

Oreet Meital, born in 1957, has a bachelor's degree in Film and Television from Tel-Aviv University and a master's in Hebrew Literature from Ben-Gurion University in the Negev. She is currently writing her PhD dissertation on the poetry of Hebrew poet Uri Zvi Greenberg. Her first poetry book, *Balance Problems* (Sifriat Poalim, 1999), was the recipient of the Education and Culture Minister's Award for First Books. Her second book, *Songs of Choice*, was published in 2007 by Carmel Press. Meital is a lecturer in Hebrew literature at Ben-Gurion University.

Agi Mishol was born in Transylvania, Romania, and brought to Israel as a very young child. She is the author of twelve books of poetry and the winner of every major Israeli poetry prize, including the first Yehuda Amichai Prize in 2002 and the Dolitsky Prize in 2007. A collection of her work in English, *Look There* (Graywolf Press), was published in 2006; volumes in Romanian and French are forthcoming. Poet in residence in 2007–2008 at the Hebrew University in Jerusalem and lecturer in literature at Alma College, Mishol holds bachelor's and master's degrees in Hebrew literature from Hebrew University. She lives on a farm near Gedera, Israel.

Mei-Tal Nadler, born in 1979, is a poet, publicist, editor, literary critic, and activist for social justice. She lives in Tel-Aviv and is studying for her master's in literature at Tel-Aviv University. Her poems have been published in all the major Israeli literary journals, including the newspaper literary supplements. She was one of the winners of the 2006 Tel-Aviv competition Poetry on the Road. Presently, she is producing a poetry performance that includes original music set to the work of well-known poets, together with poems from her forthcoming first collection.

Tal Nitzan, *see* Editors.

Amir Or was born in Tel Aviv in 1956. He has published eight poetry books, many of which have been translated into English and other languages. He has also published several books of translations from ancient Greek, Latin, and English into Hebrew. Or is the editor and artistic director of *Helicon Poetry Society*, its Hebrew-Arabic school, its journal of contemporary Hebrew poetry, and its international poetry festival. He serves as national coordinator for Poets for Peace.

Yosef Ozer, born in Jerusalem in 1952, is an ultra-orthodox Jew, affiliated with the religious literary journal *Meishiv Haruach*. Ozer has published two poetry collections and has received several awards, including the Prime Minister's Prize in 1993.

Yoram Levy Porat (1939–2006), poet, children's writer, playwright, and director, was born in Tel-Aviv. He published two plays, two children's collections, and three poetry collections, the last being *Life Is a Local Affair* (Keshev Le'Shira Press, 2007). His plays have been produced in Israel and abroad, including a premier of his play *Amerika*, a tribute to Franz Kafka, at the Kennedy Center in Washington D.C. Porat was the recipient of numerous awards and recognitions, including the Levi Eshkol Award in 2006.

Dahlia Ravikovitch (1936–2005), born in a suburb of Tel-Aviv, was a salient and central voice of contemporary Israeli poetry. She began publishing when she was eighteen, and her first book, *Love of the Golden Apple* (1959), won her immediate acclaim. In addition to eleven volumes of poetry, including three anthologizing selected poems, Ravikovitch also published three collections of short stories and a number of children's books. She was awarded many prizes, including the Bialik Prize (1987) and the Israel Prize (1998). Ravikovitch's poetry is known for its active protest against the Israeli occupation of Palestinian lands. *"Hovering at a Low Altitude": The Collected Poetry of Dahlia Ravikovitch* (translated by Chana Bloch and Chana Kronfeld) was published by Norton in 2008.

Asher Reich was born in 1937 to an ultra-orthodox Jerusalem family. At eighteen he joined the army, an act unheard of in his immediate environment. Later he studied Philosophy and Literature at the Hebrew University and left religion behind. Reich has published twelve books of poetry and has won many literary awards, including the Brenner and Bernstein Prizes, the Prime Minister's Prize in 1989, and the President's Award in 2000. His novel *Reminiscences of an Amnesiac* was published in 1992 (Maariv Press), and his collection of short stories, *Man with a Door*, was published in 2003 (Kibbutz HaMeuchad Press).

Diti Ronen, born in 1952 in Tel-Aviv, is the author of two poetry books: *Inner Moon, Notebook* (Hakibbutz Hame'uhad, 2002) and *With the Slip Showing* (Gvanim, 1999). She received her PhD from the Department of Theatre Arts, Faculty of Visual and Performing Arts, Tel Aviv University, and she was the head of the Theater and Literature departments at the Israeli Ministry of Culture from 1999 through 2006. At present, Ronen teaches and consults professionally on cultural policy and arts administration.

Tuvia Ruebner was born in 1924 in Bratislava, Slovakia, and immigrated to Palestine in 1941. His parents and sister, who stayed behind, were all murdered by the Nazis. Ruebner has published twelve books of poetry and edited a selection of masterworks in aesthetics and the entire oeuvre of poet, essayist, and playwright Lea Goldberg. Among the many European literary bodies of which he is a member, Ruebner belongs to the German Academy for Language and Literature and the Academy of Science and Literature at Mainz. He is also the recipient of many distinguished awards: in Israel he has received the Prime Minister's Award, the Jerusalem Prize, the Anne Frank Prize, the ACUM Prize, and the Israel Prize in 2008. Abroad he has received, among others, the Paul Celan Award for his translations of S. Y. Agnon. Ruebner lives on Kibbutz Merhavia.

Rami Saari, poet and translator, was born in Petah Tikva, Israel, in 1963. He studied at the universities of Helsinki, Budapest, and Jerusalem and received his PhD in Semitic languages. Saari has published seven books of poetry, the most recent being *Rings of the Years* (2008). In addition, he has translated more than forty books into Hebrew, both prose and poetry, mainly from Albanian, Finnish, Greek, Hungarian, Portuguese, and Spanish. Saari has twice won the Prime Minister's Literary Award for Poetry (1996, 2003) and was the recipient of the Tchernikhovsky Award for Translation in 2006 and the Olschwung Foundation Award in 1998. He divides his life among Greece, Israel, and Portugal.

Aharon Shabtai, born in 1939, is one of the leading poets on the Israeli literary scene. He studied Greek and Philosophy at the Hebrew University, the Sorbonne, and Cambridge, and for many years taught Theater Studies in Jerusalem. He is widely regarded as the foremost Hebrew translator of Greek drama. He is the author of eighteen books of poetry, most recently *Tanya* and *Sun, O Sun*. Two book-length selections of his work have appeared in English translations by Peter Cole: *Love & Selected Poems* (Sheep Meadow Press, 1997) and *J'Accuse* (New Directions, 2003).

Aryeh Sivan, born in Tel-Aviv in 1929, fought in Israel's 1948 War of Independence. He has published fourteen collections of poetry and one novel, *Adonis*. Sivan has been the recipient of many awards, including the prestigious Brenner Prize in 1989 and the Bialik Prize in 1998. Until retiring, Sivan taught literature and language. Many of Sivan's poems, as well as his novel, have been translated into numerous other languages. Sivan's poems in *With an Iron Pen* were first published in his book *The Hollow of the Sling*, which appeared in 1989 and focused on the Israeli-Palestinian conflict.

Ronny Someck was born in Baghdad in 1951 and came to Israel as a young child. He has published nine volumes of poetry and a book for children with his daughter Shirly (*The Laughter Button*). He has been translated into thirty-nine languages. Translated selections of his poems have appeared in Arabic, French, Catalan, Albanian, Italian, Macedonian and English. Someck is the recipient of numerous awards, including the Prime Minister's Award (1989), the Yehuda Amichai Award for Hebrew Poetry (2004), the Wine Poem Award in Struga Poetry Evenings, Macedonia (2005), and the Hans Berghhuis Prize for Poetry in the Maastricht International Poetry Nights (2006).

Tsvika Szternfeld was born in Poland in 1955 and came to Israel at the age of two. As a child he lived in Belgium and Germany and is fluent in ten languages. He has published five poetry books, the first of which (*A Reservist's Diary*, 1989) was adapted into a dance performed by the Kibbutz Dance Company. Szternfeld has won various awards and recognitions, and his poetry has been translated into French, Arabic, Polish, and Amharic. He lives in Haifa and works as a psychologist, often lecturing on intercultural relations.

Avner Treinin, born in Tel-Aviv in 1928, has lived most of his life in Jerusalem. He completed his doctorate in chemistry at the Hebrew University in Jerusalem and has taught there since, serving as the Dean of the Faculty of Natural Sciences. The recipient of a number of literary awards, including the Bialik Prize for Poetry, Treinin has published several volumes of poetry, uncollected short stories, and a critical book entitled *Between Poetry & Science: Reflections on Modern Hebrew*.

Meir Wieseltier, born in Moscow in 1941, arrived in Israel as a refugee at the age of eight. He has published twelve collections of poetry in Hebrew and won many prizes, including the prestigious Israel Prize in 2000. A collection of his poems in Italian, *Lontano Dall'Alzabandierra*, was published in Genoa in 2003. The University of California Press published his first collection in English, *The Flower of Anarchy*, translated by Shirley Kaufman, also in 2003. Since 2001 Wieselteir has been a professor in the Department of Hebrew and Comparative Literature at Haifa University.

Natan Zach was born in Berlin, Germany, in 1930, and was brought to Israel as a child. He lived in England from 1968 to 1979, where he completed his PhD at the University of Essex. Zach has published ten books of poetry, a book of short stories, two collections of essays, a memoir, and four books for children. Zach was awarded the Bialik Prize (1982), the Israel Prize (1995), the Feronia Prize (Italy, 2000), and the ACUM Prize for his life work (2003). In 2004, the

University of Geneva awarded him an honorary doctorate for his "contribution to the renewal of [Hebrew] poetry in the second half of the 20th century." Two volumes of his work have been published in English translation: *Against Parting* (1967) and *The Static Element* (1982). Zach has been on the faculty of Tel-Aviv University and Haifa University.

Translators

Rachel Tzvia Back, *see* Editors

Mark Braverman, poet, translator, and peace activist, was born in 1948 and resides in Bethesda, Maryland. He works as a psychologist, specializing in the prevention of stress and burnout in humanitarian aid workers. Braverman is the Executive Director of Friends of Tent of Nations North America, an NGO dedicated to Palestinian land rights, justice, and nonviolence in Palestine and Israel. He is also a member of the Washington Interfaith Alliance for Middle East Peace and serves on the Board of the Israeli Committee against House Demolitions—USA. He has published widely, and his work can be found at www.jewishconscience.org. Braverman's current project is a book on progressive Christian and Jewish thought on Zionism and the State of Israel.

Chana Bloch, the author of three books of poetry including the prize-winning *Mrs. Dumpty*, is cotranslator of *The Song of Songs*, Yehuda Amichai's *Selected Poetry*, and Dahlia Ravikovitch's *Dress of Fire* and *The Window*. She is the recipient (with Chana Kronfeld) of an NEA fellowship for the translation of Amichai's *Open Closed Open*, which won the PEN Translation Award. Her cotranslation (with Chana Kronfeld) of *"Hovering at a Low Altitude": The Collected Poetry of Dahlia Ravikovitch* was published by Norton in 2008.

Peter Cole's most recent book of poems is *Things on Which I've Stumbled* (New Directions). His many volumes of translations from Hebrew and Arabic include *The Dream of the Poem: Hebrew Poetry from Muslim and Christian Spain, 950– 1492* (Princeton); *So What: New & Selected Poems,* by Taha Muhammad Ali; and *J'Accuse,* by Aharon Shabtai (New Directions). Cole, who lives in Jerusalem and coedits Ibis Editions, has received numerous honors for his work, including the PEN Translation Award, a TLS translation prize, and fellowships from the NEA, the NEH, and the John Simon Guggenheim Foundation. He was recently named a MacArthur Foundation Fellow.

Vivian Sohn Eden was born in the United States. She has lived in Israel on and off since 1961 and is on the staff of *Haaretz English Edition*, a daily newspaper published in conjunction with the *International Herald Tribune*. Her articles, stories, translations, and poetry have appeared in newspapers, journals, and anthologies in the United States, Britain, Israel, and elsewhere. Among her book-length translations are the novel *Arabesques*, by Anton Shammas; *The Lords of the Land* (a study of the settlement project in the occupied territories), by Akiva Eldar and Idith Zertal; and Ahaon Megged's novel *The Flying Camel and the Golden Hump*.

Lisa Katz was born in New York and received a PhD from the English department of the Hebrew University in Jerusalem, where she has lived since 1983. *Reconstruction*, a volume of her poetry in Hebrew translation, is forthcoming from Am Oved Press in Israel. Three times nominated for a Pushcart Prize, her work appears most recently in the United States in *Hunger Mountain, Zeek, Prairie Schooner*, and *Mississippi Review* and in the anthology *Illness in the Academy* (Purdue University, 2007). *Look There: The Selected Poems of Agi Mishol* in Katz's translation was published in 2006 by Graywolf Press. She teaches literary translation and creative writing at the Hebrew University.

Shirley Kaufman was born in Seattle, lived in San Francisco, and immigrated to Jerusalem in 1973. Eight volumes of her poetry have been published in the United States, most recently *Roots in the Air: New and Selected Poems* and *Threshold* (Copper Canyon Press, 1996 and 2003). Among her many awards are two NEA grants, the Shelley Memorial Award for Lifetime Achievement from the Poetry Society of America, and the Israel President's Prize for Poetry in English in 2007. Her *Selected Poems* was published in Hebrew by Bialik Press in 1995, translated by Aharon Shabtai, and a bilingual volume of her poems was published in French by Cheyne éditeur, 2003, translated by Claude Vigeé. In 2009 Copper Canyon Press will publish Kaufman's latest collection of poems: *Ezekiel's Wheels*.

Tsipi Keller, novelist and translator, was born in Prague, raised in Israel, and has been living in the United States since 1974. She is the recipient of many awards, including a NEA Translation Fellowship and a New York Foundation for the Arts Award in fiction. Most recently, Keller is the author of the novels *Jackpot* (2004) and *Retelling* (2006), both published by Spuyten Duyvil. Her anthology, *Contemporary Hebrew Poetry*, was published by State University of New York Press in 2008.

Chana Kronfeld teaches Hebrew, Yiddish, and Comparative Literature at the University of Berkeley. Her book *On the Margins of Modernism* won the MLA Scaglione Prize in 1997 for Best Book in Comparative Literary Studies. Her cotranslation (with Chana Bloch) of Yehuda Amichai's *Open Closed Open* won the PEN Translation Award. She is the recipient (with Chana Bloch) of an NEA Fellowship for the translation of *"Hovering at a Low Altitude": The Collected Poetry of Dahlia Ravikovitch*, published by Norton in 2008.

Gabriel Levin's most recent collection of poems is *The Maltese Dreambook* (Anvil, 2008). His previous collections include *Ostraca* (Anvil, 1999) and *Sleepers of Beulah* (Sinclair-Stevenson, 1992). His translations from Hebrew and Arabic include *Poems from the Diwan*, by Yehuda Halevi (Anvil, 2002), and *So What: New and Selected Poems (With a Story) 1973–2005*, by Taha Muhammad Ali (with Peter Cole and Yahya Hijazi; Copper Canyon, 2007).

Mark Elliott Shapiro, Canadian-Israeli poet and playwright, lives in Jerusalem and has recently launched a series of chapbooks of poetry and prose. Three have already appeared. In addition to the poetry of Yosef Ozer, he has translated poems by Shaul Tchernichovsky, Avraham Huss, Jakov Steinberg, Haim Guri, and Gabriel Preil.

Editors

Rachel Tzvia Back, poet, translator, and professor of literature, has lived in Israel since 1981. Her translations of the poetry of Lea Goldberg, published in *Lea Goldberg: Selected Poetry and Drama* (Toby Press), were awarded a 2005 PEN Translation grant. Her own poetry collections are *Azimuth* (Sheep Meadow Press), *The Buffalo Poems* (Duration Press), and *On Ruins & Return: Poems 1999–2005* (Shearsman Books); her scholarly work on the poetry and poetics of Susan Howe, *Led by Language*, appeared in 2002 (University of Alabama Press). She was a 1996 recipient of the Absorption Minister's Prize for Immigrant Poets. Back is the editor and primary translator of the English version of *With an Iron Pen: Twenty Years of Hebrew Protest Poetry*. She lives in the Galilee, in the north of Israel.

Tal Nitzan, poet, editor, and translator, is one of the preeminent translators from Spanish in Israel today. Recipient of the Culture Minister's Prize for Beginning Poets in 2001, Nitzan has published three poetry books: *Domestica* (2002, Culture Minister's Prize for First Book), *An Ordinary Evening* (2006), and *Café Soleil Bleu* (2007). Her forthcoming collection, *A Short History*, won the ACUM Prize for Poetry submitted anonymously (2007). Nitzan has translated more than fifty books into Hebrew, including two anthologies of Latin American poetry. Her translations have won numerous awards, including the Culture Minister's Creation Prize for Translators (1995, 2005), and an honorary medal from Chile's president. An ardent peace activist, Nitzan edited the ground-breaking Hebrew anthology *With an Iron Pen: Hebrew Protest Poetry 1984–2004* (Xargol Books, 2005).

Index of First Lines

Index of Poems by Poet